James Lucas was
Department of
Museum.

Matthew Cooper graduated in history from London University and is a member of the House of Commons staff.

Also by James Lucas

Last Days of the Reich
Kommando
War in the Desert
Reich!

JAMES LUCAS
and MATTHEW COOPER

Hitler's Elite

Leibstandarte SS 1933–1945

GRAFTON BOOKS

A Division of the Collins Publishing Group

LONDON GLASGOW
TORONTO SYDNEY AUCKLAND

Grafton Books
A Division of the Collins Publishing Group
8 Grafton Street, London W1X 3LA

Published by Grafton Books 1990
9 8 7 6 5 4 3 2 1

First published in Great Britain by
Macdonald and Jane's
Macdonald & Co. (Publishers) Ltd 1975

A CIP catalogue record for this book is
available from the British Library

ISBN 0-586-20912-3

Printed and bound in Great Britain by
Collins, Glasgow

Set in Times

Contents

Introduction

The history of Hitler's Guard – the Leibstandarte SS 'Adolf Hitler' – is the record of a military élite, of one of the foremost fighting units of the Second World War. General Eberhard von Mackensen wrote: 'Every division wishes it had the Leibstandarte as its neighbour, as much during the attack as the defence. Its inner discipline, its cool daredevilry, its cheerful enterprise, its unshakeable firmness in a crisis . . . its exemplary toughness, its camaraderie (which deserves special praise), all these are outstanding and cannot be surpassed.' For five years, the men of the Leibstandarte fought alongside their comrades of the Waffen SS and the Wehrmacht in every major campaign on the continent of Europe, seeing action in Poland, Holland, France, the Balkans, southern USSR, Italy, Normandy, Belgium and, finally, Austria, making the journey to the Eastern Front on no less than four occasions.

But the interest of the Leibstandarte lies not only in its exploits upon the field of battle but also in its unique character. It was one of the few military formations in history whose existence was owed exclusively to the emergence of a particular political system, and whose nature reflected in microcosm the essence of the régime it served. Without Napoleon and the First Empire there would have been no Imperial Guard; without Hitler and the Third Reich there would have been no Leibstandarte.

The Leibstandarte of the mid-war years was barely recognizable from its initial form in 1933. Then it was just a handful of men in black SS uniform, but by the end of

1942 it had been transformed into a well-tried division of some 20,000 soldiers clad in field-grey. This development was in no way sudden or dramatic, nor even predetermined. Rather it was a steady progress which was closely allied to the fortunes and needs of the Leibstandarte's master – Adolf Hitler. From the first it was designed as a body of men who were exclusively the instrument of his will, entirely at his disposal in whatever area he thought fit.

Beginning as a small ideological élite concerned with protection and police duties and helping to keep order within the National Socialist Movement, the Leibstandarte's importance grew when, in mid-1934, it was required to help eliminate potential dangers to the Führer's authority. With the territorial expansion of the Third Reich it acquired new duties as a military force ready to fulfil its Führer's wishes outside the boundaries of the 'old Germany', and it took part in the several moves outward before 1939. With the outbreak of the European War came the commitment of the Leibstandarte to the field, its numbers and efficiency growing with the scale of the fighting. By 1942 it was a renowned division equipped with the best that Germany's munition factories could provide; and, as Hitler's Empire reached its zenith, his Guard was probably at the peak of its fighting ability. With the defeat of the Third Reich, however, the Leibstandarte was but a shadow of its former self, the previous years having taken enormous toll in life, limb and spirit. Just as Hitler's downfall was total, so was his Guard's. After the war, when the world realized fully the enormity that was the Third Reich, it was natural that the Leibstandarte should also be described in the darkest of terms, utterly discredited along with its creator.

Previous authors, with one or two notable exceptions,

have tended to present a one-sided picture of the Waffen SS fighting units, viewing them as an indistinguishable part of the criminal organization that was Himmler's SS. As such the Leibstandarte has received the condemnation which runs along the lines of that set out by the International Military Tribunal at Nuremberg in 1946, when it declared that the Waffen SS 'was in theory and practice as much an integral part of the SS organization as any branch of the SS'; and therefore as such was used 'for purposes which were criminal . . . including the persecution and extermination of the Jews, brutalities and killings in the concentration camps . . .'. In particular the Waffen SS was thought to have taken part 'in steps leading up to aggressive war' and to have been 'directly involved in the killing of prisoners of war and the atrocities in occupied countries. It supplied personnel for the Einsatzgruppen [extermination squads] and had command of the concentration camp guards . . .'.

On the other hand, however, there are those who seek to justify the Leibstandarte, and, in the words of General Heinz Guderian, to 'disperse the clouds of lies and calumnies piled up around the Waffen SS', and to 'help these gallant men to resume the place they deserve alongside the other branches of the Wehrmacht'. A distinguished officer of the Leibstandarte, Kurt Meyer, demanded that 'former SS troops should not be treated as second-class citizens [when] they did nothing more than fight for their country'.

The truth lies in a combination of these opposing views. The picture of the Leibstandarte that emerges is a complicated one, parts of which are near incomprehensible to those who have not lived through the era of National Socialist Germany. But there is always evident the fact that Hitler's Guard provided the Third Reich with a valuable fighting force whose prowess as a front-line unit was second to none. As its own propaganda declared: 'We want to be the best . . ., because this performance is expected of us . . .'.

Acknowledgements

In the preparation of this book the authors have been greatly assisted by many, and they would like to take this opportunity to express their warm gratitude to the following:

L. Klein; D. E. Ascher; B. Calder; T. Charman; L. Milner; T. Scott and to Mrs B. Shaw. Particular thanks must go to Miss E. Austin; A. B. Edwards; and M. Stevens of Macdonald and Jane's for their valuable help and advice.

The photographs are reproduced with kind permission of A. Mollo; B. L. Davis; M. Shaw; L. Milner; C. Hesse; F. L. Förster; and the Imperial War Museum.

The fact that two authors were engaged upon the preparation of this work caused nearly as many difficulties as it solved, and there inevitably arose the necessity for specialization. In order to avoid any confusion and to explain variations in style, it is as well to indicate that James Lucas was responsible for the military operations, while Matthew Cooper dealt with all other aspects of the book.

The authors would like to record their indebtedness to former soldiers and next of kin of fallen men of the 1st SS Panzer Division for permission to quote, either verbatim or as a paraphrase, from personal letters and a diary.

Note:

SS ranks in the German vernacular have been used throughout the text. Appendix 1 gives, as far as possible, their British and US equivalents.

'Leibstandarte' is pronounced 'Libestandarter'.

1

Political Background

The origins of the Leibstandarte go back to the first years of the National Socialist Party (NSDAP), to a time when Hitler was still leader of an obscure Bavarian political organization. Formed in March 1923, the Stabswache (Headquarters Guard) consisted of just two men – Joseph Berchtold and Julius Schreck – sworn to protect Hitler from all enemies, with their lives if necessary. This was an important development for the Party and, eventually, for Germany, since it established for the first time a force which was entirely at Hitler's disposal, whose existence was concerned solely with his will and safety.

The Stabswache was short-lived, however. It was succeeded in May by the Stosstrupp 'Adolf Hitler' (Shock Troop), composed initially of some thirty men under Berchtold's command. In Hitler's words: 'Being convinced that there are always circumstances in which élite troops are called for, I created . . . the Shock Troop "Adolf Hitler". It was made up of men who were ready for revolution and who knew that someday things would come to hard knocks.' Its members appeared to enjoy a good fight, and were always ready to do their leader's bidding with their 'indiarubbers' (rubber truncheons) and 'matchboxes' (pistols). During the abortive Munich Putsch of 9th November 1923, they performed loyal but destructive service, some accompanying Hitler while others ransacked the offices of the social-democratic paper 'The Munich Post'. After the failure of this attempt to seize power, Hitler was imprisoned and his Stosstrupp disbanded, to be resurrected in spirit, if not in name, some eighteen months later.

Upon his release in December 1924, Hitler felt the need of a new guard, unsure as he was of his position. 'When I came out of Landsberg everything was broken up and scattered in sometimes rival bands. I told myself then that I needed a bodyguard, even a restricted one, but made up of men who would be enlisted unconditionally, ready even to march against their own brothers, only twenty men to a city (on condition that one could count on them absolutely) rather than a dubious mass. It was Maurice, Schreck and Heiden who formed in Munich the first group of toughs . . .'. In April 1925 eight men came together to create a new Stabswache. After two weeks the unit was renamed the Schützstaffel (Protection Squad). Thus the SS was born.

The history of the SS belongs more properly to the pages of other works; suffice it to say here that it soon outgrew its original intention of being primarily a bodyguard to Hitler. By 1933 the SS had grown to an unwieldy 52,000 men and by mid-1939 to 240,000 men, its members serving in a number of diverse areas which included the secret police, counter-espionage, the concentration camps, economic enterprises, resettlement, political education and even maternity homes. Upon his assumption of power in January 1933 Hitler again felt strongly the need for a highly-trained, armed, and full-time body of men whom he could truly call his own and who could afford him the protection he so earnestly desired, but which could not be guaranteed by his few personal SS attendants, his Reichswehr guards or his police escort. Thus, for the fourth time in ten years, he instituted a guard for himself, naturally turning to his SS as he did so.

On 17th March 1933 an old Party comrade and former bodyguard, SS Gruppenführer Josef Dietrich, reported to

Hitler that he had now formed a new headquarters guard of 120 hand-picked, loyal SS men as ordered. The unit, known as the SS Stabswache 'Berlin', was quartered in the Alexander Barracks in Friedrichstrasse not far from Hitler's official residence, the Reich Chancellery.

In May the Stabswache was re-formed as SS Sonder-kommando Zossen (Special Commando) designed as an élite political paramilitary formation, which, in addition to its guard duties, could be used for armed police and anti-terrorist tasks. After four months the unit was merged with the SS Sonderkommando Jüterbog, and received its final title – SS Leibstandarte 'Adolf Hitler' – the name invoking memories of the famed Bavarian Life Guards. The occasion upon which this was announced was 3rd September 1933 during the Nuremberg Rally, 'Congress of Victory'. After a speech which lasted eighty minutes Hitler introduced his new Guard, one American eye-witness writing that 'It was a long time to wait for the unrewarding fact that a few toughs were now given the official title SS Bodyguard Regiment "Adolf Hitler".' Two months later, on 9th November, in front of the hallowed Feldherrnhalle War Memorial, before which, exactly ten years previously, the Munich Putsch had met its end, the Leibstandarte took an oath of loyalty unto death to its Führer.

From its inception the Leibstandarte was a part of the SS, which itself was, from July 1934, an independent formation within the NSDAP. According to the Party's Organization Book 'the original and most important duty of the SS is to serve as the protector of the Führer', but 'by decree . . . its sphere of duties has been enlarged to include the internal security of the Reich'. As will be seen later, the Leibstandarte included both roles within its field of activity. As an SS unit it came under the overall control of Heinrich Himmler as Reichsführer SS, and was administered by the SS Hauptamt (the SS Main Office which was formed in mid-1935). However, in practice there was the important qualification that the Leibstandarte was Hitler's own Guard, and that the Führer considered himself to be the ultimate director of its actions. To this was added Dietrich's friendship with, and close proximity to, Hitler, something which the Guard commander was prepared to exploit to the full. As a consequence the Leibstandarte enjoyed a fair measure of independence within the SS.

This was summed up in a letter written by the Führer to Himmler in 1938: 'Dietrich is master in his own house, which, I would remind you, is my house.' On one occasion Dietrich roundly turned upon the Reichsführer SS during a discussion, telling him: 'My position as guard commander will no more allow your interference on security matters than it will upon the morality of my men. They are mine and we are his [Hitler's]. Now go back to your office and let us get on with the job.'

Few indeed were the SS men who could speak thus to Himmler. During the war Dietrich even managed to protect one of his men from a revengeful security chief – Heydrich – no mean feat! The Leibstandarte was, in Himmler's words 'a complete law unto itself. It does and allows anything it likes without taking the slightest notice of orders from above.' When one considers that the SS was regarded as the élite order within the Third Reich, the position Dietrich and his men had evolved for themselves was indeed truly aristocratic.

The Leibstandarte was naturally closely concerned with Hitler's safety. From the Berlin-Lichterfelde barracks (into which Dietrich's unit had moved in late 1933) squads of men were sent to the Reich Chancellery, there to provide a smart and efficient guard for the Führer. The

Leibstandarte came to be in exclusive prominence around the Führer, its men serving not only as Hitler's guards but also as his adjutants, drivers, servants and waiters. At the Berghof, his mountain retreat, the Leibstandarte was less in evidence but just as active nevertheless, providing security for an area some 2.7 miles square. During the war the protection duties were increased, and, after the July Bomb Plot in 1944, it became so intensive that young Leibstandarte officers would search even Generals before allowing them near Hitler.

On 27th June 1934, 'Sepp' Dietrich asked the Reichswehr authorities for arms to enable the Leibstandarte to carry out a 'secret and most important mission ordered by the Führer'. This was to be the first occasion when Hitler's Guard was required to prove itself as an instrument of his will. The particular causes of the so-called 'Night of the Long Knives' have no place here, it being enough to know that by this time the conflicts within Germany had reached such a pitch that something had to happen. On 28th June the final decision was taken to eliminate the leadership of the powerful and potentially dangerous SA (Stormtroopers), Hitler declaring 'I have had enough. I shall make an example of them.' The consequence was that the SS, according to Himmler, '. . . did not hesitate . . . to do the duty we were bidden, and stand comrades who had lapsed up against the wall and shoot them'.

The Leibstandarte, owing to the trust placed upon it, was to have the central role in the whole operation. It was planned that two companies would move down to southern Bavaria and there, aided by concentration camp guards, take prisoner the assembled SA leaders at the Bad Wiesee resort. Accordingly, early on the morning of the 29th the Leibstandarte was put on the alert, and that evening Dietrich reported to his Führer.

However, as events turned out, the Leibstandarte was

not used precisely as planned. Hitler, out of anger, fear
and impatience, carried out the arrests himself early on
the morning of the 30th, while his Guards were still on
the road. But that evening, at 17.00 hours, Dietrich was
instructed by Hitler to select one officer and half a dozen
men to provide the execution squad for six prominent SA
leaders. One hour later he arrived at the Stadelheim
prison with 'six good shots to ensure that nothing messy
happened', and after some delay, due to objections raised
by the prison governor, the shooting went ahead. The
men were led out one by one into the grey prison
courtyard. There they were confronted by the firing squad
drawn up in line abreast and received by a polite Leibstandarte officer with the words 'The Führer and Reich
Chancellor has condemned you to death. The sentence
will be carried out forthwith.' Then, with efficiency and
no mess, they were shot, one after the other. Dietrich,
however, could not preserve the same air of detachment
as his men, and, as he said later, 'Before it was Schnei-
dhuber's turn I was off. I had had enough.'

In Berlin the Leibstandarte was considerably more
active. It had been ordered to form a number of Action
Commandos (Einsatzkommandos) to act with other SS
units against 'enemies of the State'. These mobile squads
were let loose on the streets of the capital on mid-morning
of the 30th, one local police report talking of their 'hit
and run raids of extreme violence'. One such group,
eighteen strong and commanded by the tough and unprin-
cipled SS Hauptsturmführer Kurt Gildisch, was responsible for the brutal murder of Klausner, a Director in the
Transport Ministry and President of the Catholic Action.
At 13.00 hours Gildisch shot Klausner in his office as his
back was turned, and then faked a suicide, leaving as
unconcerned as he had entered.

Many of those the SS arrested were taken to the

Lichterfelde barracks which had become a disposal area for unwanted people and corpses. It is not known just how many were shot by the Leibstandarte firing squads, nor who was in command, but it is thought that there were some forty executioners who performed their duty in a somewhat amateurish way. It has been stated that 150 people were stood against the wall at the Lichterfelde, but this is probably an overestimate. The shooting finally ended early on 2nd July; the Leibstandarte's first action was over. As Hitler later stated: 'In this hour I was the supreme judge of the German people.' In this hour, too, his Guard had been the supreme executioner.

Since the SS, in Himmler's words, guaranteed 'the security of Germany from the interior' it was almost inevitable that in order to complement its activities in areas such as the secret police and the concentration camp guards, it should develop an armed force designed for anti-terrorist 'heavy police' tasks during periods of internal strife. The nucleus for this was already at hand in the form of the SS Politische Bereitschaften (Political Readiness Squads) which were full-time, armed units of at least company strength trained for such duties. It was as a Politische Bereitschaft that the Leibstandarte was classified, trained, and in June 1934 used. After this date, free at last from the restricting tutelage of the SA, reinforced in prestige, and confirmed in its usefulness, the SS was able to forge ahead in its development. As a part of this, the armed SS units were now reorganized and expanded, and the Leibstandarte was increased to regimental strength by the end of October. In December Himmler ordered that the Politische Bereitschaften be formed into battalions and integrated more fully with the Leibstandarte; and the following year, on 16th March 1935, Hitler announced that these units were now officially established and known collectively as the SS Verfügungstruppe – SS-VT – (literally 'For Disposal Troops' but best translated as 'Special Purpose Troops'). Now, as an SS-VT unit, the Leibstandarte increasingly evolved a new role, transforming from a purely political police unit into a military force.

To understand this somewhat confusing development it is necessary to look at the oath sworn by the assembled Leibstandarte men in front of the Feldherrnhalle in November 1933, and subsequently by every man who entered the ranks of the armed SS: 'I swear to you, Adolf Hitler, as Führer and Reich Chancellor, loyalty and bravery. I vow to you, and those you have named to command me, obedience unto death. So help me God.'

While it was not generally recognized at the time, this oath held great significance for the future. Through his title of Führer of the NSDAP and Reich Chancellor (and, after the death of Hindenburg in 1934, the office, but not the title, of President) Hitler laid claim to complete sovereignty over the German people. This was buttressed and extended by the belief in his 'historic mission', which ensured that he was not to be bound by any existing law or code of morality. The Leibstandarte was the servant of such a master. This is the key to an understanding of the Leibstandarte's position within the political and military structure of the Third Reich. In the words of one historian, Hans Buchheim, the formation of Hitler's Guard on such principles was 'one of the first steps in constituting the authority of the Führer as an independent factor in German public life – the Reich Chancellor had formed a body of armed men who had no place in the State or the Party organizations, but was at the sole disposal of the Führer and pledged to him personally. Hitler had to render account to no one for the use to which these men were put, and no other than he had power of command over them.' Such was the status of the Leibstandarte:

complete and unconditional obedience to the Führer who was himself above all restriction – a Praetorian Guard indeed!

Such also was the position of the whole of the armed SS. The nature and implications of the oath meant that the SS-VT could be used in any role Hitler chose, and that its employment as an élite unit might well vary with the particular problems which confronted him at any given time. Thus in 1934 the Leibstandarte could be sent against his internal enemies in a police action, and in 1939 against his external enemies in a military role. Therefore the growth of the early SS-VT, with a strength of 8,459 men in May 1935, into the later Waffen SS, numbering some 594,000 men in June 1944, must be seen not as one of political design to undermine the Army's position, but rather as one of necessity dictated by the course of events.

Despite the many claims to the contrary, Hitler never intended to build up the armed SS to the point it later reached, nor did he have any ideas of it either replacing or even rivalling the Army in military importance. It is quite probable that when, in August 1934, he assured the armed forces that they were to be 'the sole bearer of arms' in Germany's external affairs, he did not foresee any development to the contrary. Even Himmler, ever anxious to expand the sphere of his responsibilities, was prepared in 1936 to leave it to the Wehrmacht to guarantee the 'safety of the honour, the greatness and the peace of the Reich from the exterior'.

As was made clear, the SS was to have 'a standing armed force for such special internal tasks as may be allotted to the SS by the Führer'. Hitler's intention was that the SS-VT was to be 'a militarized force ready for police action within the Reich boundaries when the dissident forces are too strong for the normal security services'. From the start, the military were to be allowed a fair degree of control over the SS-VT – the Army, being responsible for military training, was granted the right of inspection and the budgetary checking of the units, and was guaranteed that, in the event of war, the SS-VT formations would be dispersed among the armed forces and placed under their command. The High Command could also in effect control the numerical strength of the SS-VT through the manpower allocation rights of the Defence District Headquarters, and it made full use of this privilege. (The Wehrmacht retained a goodly proportion – sometimes as high as two-thirds – of those desirous and capable of joining the armed SS.)

However, it was but a relatively short step from being equipped and trained for anti-terrorist, 'heavy police' duties to being organized for military, warlike activities. With the transference of Hitler's attention from internal to external affairs came a similar development in the SS-VT. As the Chief of the Army General Staff, Ludwig Beck noted: 'It was interesting to observe that an organization, which Hitler had categorically stated would never bear arms in military operations, was now taking part in every coup the Führer pulled off. Not only were they taking part, but they were, by 1938, wearing Army uniform instead of their own, except on ceremonial occasions.' On 7th March 1936 the Leibstandarte played a leading role in Hitler's first move outwards, when it provided the advance guard in the occupation of the demilitarized zone of the Rhineland. To his hesitant generals Hitler had proclaimed: 'If the Army is reluctant to lead the way, a suitable spearhead will be provided by the Leibstandarte.' At dawn on the 7th a company of Hitler's Guards moved across the Rhine and proceeded unopposed to Saarbrücken on the border with France. A local newspaper somewhat over-enthusiastically greeted their arrival with the words: 'Hitler's Men – they are gods come to show us the way for the new Germany.'

Two years later, almost to the day, Germany and the Leibstandarte were again on the march, this time into Austria. On the morning of 12th March 1938 a battalion of Hitler's Guard, having come straight from Berlin, crossed the border of the Reich near Passau as the rearguard of General Guderian's XVI Army Corps. It moved through Linz, where it provided a guard of honour for Hitler, and on to Vienna, which it reached early on the morning of the 13th. There it took its appropriate place in the triumphal celebrations, staying in the area until April when it returned to its quarters. The whole operation had meant that the Leibstandarte battalion covered no less than 600 miles in some forty-eight hours in full co-operation with the Army. Hitler's Guard had revealed a surprisingly high military ability and had earned the favourable recognition of no less a commander than General Guderian.

Seven months later the Leibstandarte took part in its last exercise of power before the war – the occupation of the Sudetenland on 3rd October 1938. Little of note occurred, the whole operation proceeding smoothly. After providing part of the guard of honour for Hitler at Carlsbad, the Leibstandarte returned to Berlin to under-take its final period of training before entering upon its first battles.

At the same time as the SS-VT was taking part in Germany's expansion, there were other disturbing developments which appeared to be upsetting the Wehrmacht's position as 'sole arms bearer'. From May 1935, membership of the SS-VT was regarded as military service with the armed forces, and in October 1936 the armed SS had acquired its own General Staff in the form of the SS-VT

Inspectorate under the command of Paul Hausser, an ex-Reichswehr Lieutenant-General. (The Inspectorate was replaced in 1940 by the SS Führungsamt – the Main Operational Office.) Improvements in equipment, numbers and training continued, and this, coupled with the influx of many able ex-Army officers, considerably heightened the military complexion of the SS-VT. In November 1937, Himmler was able to declare, perhaps a little prematurely, that 'the Verfügungstruppe is, according to the present standards of the Wehrmacht, prepared for war.' Such was the position that General Fritsch, the Commander-in-Chief of the Army, voiced the fears of many when he wrote in early 1938: '. . . it is the Verfügungstruppe which, expanded further and further, must create an opposition to the Army, simply through its existence. Even though the Army does have a certain right of inspection with regard to the training of the SS Verfügungstruppe, this SS unit develops itself totally apart, and, it appears to me, in deliberate opposition to the Army. All units report unanimously that the relationship of the SS Verfügungstruppe to the Army is very cool, if not hostile.'

By 1938 events had clearly taken the two sides to the point where they appeared to be rivals. In many ways this was an artificial antagonism, for it was not Hitler's intention to have his armed SS compete in role or numbers with the Army. Therefore, on 17th August 1938 he issued an instruction outlining the position of the SS-VT and clarifying its relationship with the armed forces. He laid down that the SS-VT 'forms no part of the Wehrmacht nor of the police. It is a permanent armed force at my disposal.' As 'a formation of the NSDAP' it was to be 'recruited and trained in ideological and political matters by the Reichsführer SS in accordance with the directives given by me'. In case of emergency 'the SS-VT will be used for two purposes: 1) By the Commander-in-Chief of the Army within the framework of the Army. It will then be subject exclusively to military law and instructions; politically, however, it will remain a branch of the NSDAP. 2) At home in case of emergency in accordance with my instructions. It will then be under the orders of the Reichsführer SS . . .'.

This was the position of the armed SS, and although it gained judicial freedom from the Wehrmacht in 1939, it never acquired any further significant independence, and continued to remain firmly under the operational control of the Wehrmacht until the end of the war. Nor did the substantial growth and commitment to battle of the Waffen SS (Armed SS) change Hitler's ultimate intention for his 'militarized State police'. (Waffen SS was the title which succeeded that of the SS-VT, the first official use of which was on 1st December 1939. It was used exclusively after 22nd April 1941.)

In August 1940 Hitler emphasized this position in his 'Statement on the Future of the Armed State Police' which was summarized and circulated to Army commands:

'In its final form the Greater German Reich will include within its frontiers peoples who will not necessarily be well-disposed towards the Reich. Outside the borders of the Old Reich, therefore, it will be necessary to create an armed State police capable, whatever the situation, of representing and enforcing the authority of the Reich in the interior of the country concerned.

'This duty can only be carried out by a State police containing within its ranks men of the best German blood and identified unquestionably with the ideology upon which the Greater German Reich is founded. Only a formation constituted upon these lines will be able to resist subversive influences in times of crisis . . .

'The Waffen SS formations will return home having proved

themselves in the field and so will have the authority required to carry out their duties as State police. Such use of the Waffen SS at home is in the interests of the Wehrmacht itself . . . In order to ensure that the quality of the men in the Waffen SS always remains high, the number of units must remain limited . . . and should, in general, not exceed 5 to 10 per cent of the peacetime strength of the Army.'

Even at the end of 1944, when the Waffen SS had grown to some 600,000 men and included no less than seven Panzer divisions within its order of battle, Hitler was able to declare that its heavy casualties 'will mould and train the survivors for their demanding security tasks in the post-war years'. Thus the commitment to the field of the SS-VT in 1939 was not caused by the conscious adoption of a new role by the armed SS. Rather it was in response to Hitler's need for field troops at that particular time, just as the considerable expansion of the Waffen SS after 1942 was due not to the Führer's desire to supplant the Army by a political force, but to his then pressing requirement for élite fighting divisions.

From its inception the Leibstandarte had embarked upon military training as an integral part of its protection and 'heavy police' duties. The SS Sonderkommandos Jüterbog and Zossen had trained on the military manoeuvre areas of the same name, and from September 1933 the 9th Infantry Regiment (appropriately enough the descendant of the old Imperial 1st Foot Guards) took control of the Leibstandarte's military endeavours. But despite the high state of fitness enjoyed by the men of the Leibstandarte, little real progress was made. The nature of its guard and ceremonial duties was not conducive to a strict military training programme. Allied to this, Dietrich and his officers had no desire to undertake any such exhaustive and distracting procedures, nor to allow outside interference by so doing. Therefore the Leibstandarte, although an SS-VT formation, took little notice of the newly formed SS-VT Inspectorate. This resulted in many clashes between Dietrich and Hausser. As late as 1938 the chief of the SS Hauptamt wrote that 'If, contrary to all orders, instructions and assurances, the Leibstandarte chooses to act in this arbitrary manner, I foresee great difficulties.' Himmler, writing to Dietrich, implored him: 'For the last time I ask you to stop these things. I can no more admit to the Wehrmacht that I am unable to get the Leibstandarte to conform to my orders and instructions valid for the entire Verfügungstruppe than I can tolerate continuance of these extravagances.' But it was to little avail. By 1936 Himmler had come to accept at least a measure of the Leibstandarte's independence, wisely allowing that the inspection of Hitler's Guard was his own prerogative, and that Hausser was merely 'authorized to attend Leibstandarte parades'. The gates of the Lichterfelde remained firmly closed to unwanted outside interference.

As the SS-VT developed and increased its military efficiency the Leibstandarte was shown up by comparison. The rest of the SS-VT contemptuously referred to its members as the 'Asphalt Soldiers' – a reference to their propensity to stamp about the parade ground and do little else. A foremost armed SS soldier, Felix Steiner, commented to a friend: 'It's pathetic. If the Führer realized what his blond gods can't do he would get rid of the lot of them.' A rather more critical than usual Leibstandarte NCO wrote early in 1936: 'The men can handle a rifle all right, but little else. If you told them to assault a strongpoint they would probably bunch together and run at it hoping that the combination of noise and numbers would suffice. Some have never even practised fire and movement. We are smart enough and tough enough, but there's a long way to go.'

There was indeed, but it is surprising just how quickly

the Leibstandarte developed into a first-class military unit and how far it assimilated itself within the armed SS. This appears to have been due to the fortuitous conjunction of several factors over two or three years which laid the foundation of the Leibstandarte's military strength. Firstly, there was the potential which Hitler's Guard already possessed – the physical quality of its members, its high morale and aggressive spirit, and, of course, its commander, Dietrich – a first-class leader. Secondly, the Reich was expanding and needed a military force, and the Leibstandarte inevitably wished to be in on the act. Thirdly, there was the infusion of new officers from the excellent SS training schools. Fourthly, there was the influence of Hausser and Steiner which had done so much to develop the military efficiency of the rest of the SS-VT. And fifthly, there was the realization by Dietrich and his senior officers that the Leibstandarte was not being taken seriously by the soldiers and other SS men. Thus from 1938 Hausser was allowed considerably greater authority and supervision over the military affairs of the Leibstandarte, Dietrich going so far as to allow an exchange of company and battalion commanders between his unit and the rest of the SS-VT. One or two officers were even sent to train with Army formations. However, it needed the shared triumphs and tribulations of war to finally weld the various armed SS formations together. In 1941 the chief of the SS Hauptamt could write: 'Nothing more remains of the former exclusiveness of the Leibstandarte. Their battle experience has had a wonderfully maturing effect.'

Contact between the armed SS and the Wehrmacht varied considerably between the harmonious and the stormy. From the beginning there was a spirit of rivalry between the two, the soldiers indignant at what they considered to be political upstarts and fearful of their future development, while the SS men were aggressive in their claims and resentful of the Army's attitude and undoubted military strength. Both appeared contemptuous of each other. In 1938 Fritsch wrote: 'One cannot help forming the impression that the hostile attitude towards the Army is blatantly encouraged within the SS-Verfügungstruppe. This hostility finds its expression in the failure of many SS men to salute officers.' Before 1939 especially, brawls between members of the Army and the SS-VT were not uncommon, the sentences passed on the offenders by their officers often being noticeably lenient. An SS report spoke of 'the social reserve of the Army officers, and the open aggression of their men, which sours all our efforts to the contrary'.

During the war this hostility continued, although it significantly abated as time proceeded. Early on even the Chief of the SS Hauptamt was forced to admit of the Leibstandarte that they took their SS spirit 'to ultimate extremes. They behave as if they have the ear of God Almighty as well as His blessing.' It was not unknown for the Waffen SS completely to disregard the commands of its Army superiors, the High Command accusing Dietrich in 1941 of 'charging into Rostov . . . purely to gain a prestige victory' entirely against orders. General Blaskowitz was so disgusted at the Leibstandarte commander's looting in Poland that he took the brave and unusual step of attempting to court-martial him.

Nor did Field-Marshal Rommel have much time for the Waffen SS, recording that 'wherever the SS men were, there was looting and brutality, and it was impossible even to discipline their ordinary soldiers'. He considered the Leibstandarte to be 'a law unto themselves'. 'I remember once in Italy I had cause to complain about the Leibstandarte's looting. Soon afterwards Dietrich, knowing I was a very enthusiastic philatelist, sent me a magnificent collection – looted of course.'

The SS men for their part often felt themselves hard done by. One particularly common cause of complaint was that the Army commanders were attempting to destroy the Waffen SS divisions by placing them in the toughest positions of the front-line and assigning them near-impossible tasks. There was also a belief that whatever they did the Army would find fault. To assembled Leibstandarte officers in late 1940 Himmler lamented: 'Then there is the complaint from the Wehrmacht that we have heard ever since 1933. Every SS man is a potential NCO but it is a pity that their commanders are so bad. After the war in Poland they said that the SS had high casualties because they were not trained for the job. Now that we have very small losses, they suppose that we have not fought.'

However, the war did serve to bring the two rivals closer together, enabling Guderian to write: 'The longer the war lasted the more they [the Waffen SS] became part of us.' Even before 1939, the co-operation between the two in the various expansions of the Reich, the links engendered by military training, and the fact that many SS-VT officers were retired soldiers and thus had direct contacts with the Army, caused a closer, pleasanter intercourse to evolve. In June 1939, the Commander-in-Chief of the Army, von Brauchitsch, issued a directive proclaiming that it was necessary for 'a mutual relationship of trust and comradeship to be developed, which is the prerequisite for partnership in battle'. This was to be done through SS participation in Army exercises and courses, regular social connections between the two officer corps, and publicity of the close collaboration in the national press.

In general it is true to say that the more the Waffen SS and the Wehrmacht came into contact one with another, the better their relations became. The Army came to realize that the armed SS was not composed solely of Nazi toughs, while the SS increasingly found military men and ways to its liking.

A mutual respect and trust was developed upon the battlefield, the value of the Waffen SS divisions being recognized as much by their reliability in defeat as by their contribution to victory.

Some generals had nothing but the highest praise for the armed SS, von Mackensen being confident that the Leibstandarte enjoyed 'an outstanding reputation not only with its superior officers, but also among its Army comrades'. It was, he wrote in 1941: 'A genuine élite military formation that I am happy to have under my command and, furthermore, one that I sincerely and hopefully wish to retain. This unrestrained recognition was gained by the Leibstandarte entirely on the basis of its own achievements, and, moreover, on the basis of its military ability against an enemy [the Russians] whose courage, toughness, numbers and armaments should not be slighted. The aura which naturally surrounds the Führer's Guard would not have sufficed, here at the front, to allow this recognition to fall into its lap.'

As the war continued, the Waffen SS became increasingly detached from its political background, and developed into an organization which was not just pro-Army but was in many ways almost exclusively military in outlook and performance. There was much sympathy evident between the Waffen SS and Wehrmacht field commanders, this affinity spreading throughout the rank and file, so that, although praise was often only grudgingly given by the Armed Forces High Command, much evidence exists of comradely actions between the former rivals. Dietrich, for example, came to enjoy a good understanding with many Army officers (something which would have appeared inconceivable in the 1930s); General Geyr von Schweppenburg found him both 'complaisant and comradely', and von Kluge described him as a colleague 'whom I have come to know and appreciate as a brave and incorruptible man in these difficult weeks'. Perhaps the last word should be given to Field-Marshal von Manstein. Although he was to write that the SS 'paid a toll of blood incommensurate with its actual gains', he nevertheless recognized that 'in no circumstances must we forget, however, that the Waffen SS, like the good comrades they were, fought shoulder to shoulder with the Army at the front and always showed themselves courageous and reliable'.

Finally, it has often been alleged that the Waffen SS in some way constituted a part of the Wehrmacht. However, this is not accurate. It is an erroneous impression originating from the aspirations of Himmler and a circle of senior SS officers who saw the armed SS as a 'Fourth Arm'. For, although the Waffen SS fought alongside the armed forces and came under Wehrmacht control in the field (as did units of the Reich Labour Service, for example), there were basic differences arising out of conception, design, history, organization, and spirit which set it apart. The Wehrmacht owed its allegiance to the State; the armed SS to Hitler.

2
Unit Character

What made the élite armed SS units particularly potent in battle was their attitude towards fighting, a spirit inculcated in all training, and cultivated whenever possible. An American officer who had fought against Peiper's Battle Group recorded: 'These men revealed a form of fighting that is new to me. They are obviously soldiers but they fight as if military ways were of no consequence . . . They actually seem to enjoy combat for no other reason than that it is combat.' It was remarked by more than one observer that the members of the Waffen SS were 'not soldiers but fighters' – men whose attitude to war was one of basic behaviour rather than of military practice. This found its philosophical expression in the distinctly dubious doctrine of 'heroic realism', the essence of which according to Werner Best was 'to fight a good fight; whether it is for a "good cause" or whether it is successful matters little'. One SS Hauptsturmführer summed up what this meant for him when he wrote: 'It was those defensive battles of the winter 1941–42 which I shall always remember, rather than the victorious advance, for the sheer beauty [Erhabenheit] of the fighting. Many of us died horribly, some even as cowards, but for those who lived even for a short period out there, it was well worth all the dreadful suffering and danger. After a time we got to a point when we were not concerned for ourselves, or even for Germany, but lived entirely for the next clash, the next engagement with the enemy. There was a tremendous sense of "being", an exhilarating feeling that every nerve in the body was alive to the fight.'

This fighting for fighting's sake had turned the soldierly concept into one of pure belligerence. It gave to both the leaders and the led a distinctive bravado and hardness in action which enabled them to face the prospect of almost certain death with an equanimity unknown to most soldiers. As Himmler put it when discoursing upon the Leibstandarte's heavy losses: 'Their lives are of value to them only as long as they can be used to serve the Führer . . . they toss them away for all the world as if they were hand-grenades when the need, or even the opportunity, arises.' The historian Eugen Kogen summed it up when he wrote: 'There was much naïve and boyish idealism in the ranks of the Waffen SS coupled with a savage soldier-of-fortune spirit'; and, although the men 'knew little or nothing concrete about the SS superstate or about SS aims' they concentrated on 'the realization of a single SS ideal – a tough recklessness. To them this was the epitome of the SS.'

Added to this, there was the spirit enshrined in the SS motto: 'My Loyalty is My Honour' which above all else was supposed in theory to form the basis of the SS's actions. Dietrich expressed it thus: 'We ask for and give complete loyalty to the Führer and to those he has set above us. To you recruits I say that even the smallest wish expressed by one of your NCOs must be interpreted as an order from the Führer. Just as you will render complete and uncircumscribed loyalty to Hitler and the National Socialist Movement, so will the Leibstandarte fulfil its duties.' Loyalty and obedience were regarded as one; the SS instructing that 'obedience must be unconditional. It corresponds to the conviction that National Socialist ideology must reign supreme . . . Every SS man, therefore, is prepared to carry out unhesitatingly any order issued by the Führer or a superior, regardless of the sacrifice involved.' As a direct result of this sprang the idea of achievement, that nothing was to be considered impossible. In Himmler's words: 'I must repeat – the word "impossible" must never be heard in the SS. It is unthinkable, gentlemen, that anyone should report to his superior "I cannot arrange this or that" or "I cannot do it with so few people" or "my battalion is not trained" or "I feel myself incapable". Gentlemen, that kind of reaction is simply not permitted . . . It is unthinkable that we should one day say to the Führer "We have no more to offer, my Führer".' Thus an order from a superior was regarded as a command from Hitler, its execution brooking no obstacle, its fulfilment being above life itself. This gave to the Waffen SS its distinctive ruthlessness, steadfastness and thoroughness in combat, its members believing that the end fully justified the means.

Yet another aspect of the Leibstandarte's character was its easy camaraderie, a feature which much impressed all who came in contact with the Waffen SS. It was a communal spirit not far removed from that traditionally fostered in the English public schools and epitomized in the phrase 'all for one and one for all'. A close relationship was formed between leaders and led, built up on the games field, and in the mess. There was not the usual officer corps exclusiveness to be found in the armed SS, due to a large extent to the fact that the majority had served in the ranks before their promotion. Instead of the strict forms of address standard in the Wehrmacht, a man might ask an officer: 'May I speak to you as a man of the Leibstandarte?', and conversation between them was encouraged, Dietrich and his fellow officers often dining with the other ranks. This comradeship, this solidarity between the men, strengthened by the shared experiences of war, coupled with the high degree of leadership manifested by the officers ensured that despite all losses and defeats the Leibstandarte would continue as a coherent fighting force until the very end. The diary entry of a tank crewman sums it up: 'To-day "Heini" was killed [his commander]. Words cannot express the grief we all feel. He has given us so much. He led us as befitted his qualities, but lived as one of us. Hard on the parade-ground and in the field, he nevertheless revealed a care, consideration and friendliness towards us that we repaid in full. I have literally seen men die for him.'

In conclusion, the Leibstandarte, even more than the other dozen or so élite Waffen SS divisions, considered itself to be, as Hitler's Guard, a formation apart from and above all others. In SS Obergruppenführer Jüttner's words, it formed 'a tightly knit aristocracy of manhood, whose special service to the Führer combines with the strongest of SS and military ideals to create a perfect political fighting machine'. It was this that proved the great attraction to the men who joined, the belief that thereby they were stretching themselves both physically and mentally, that the qualifications and code of conduct demanded marked them out as true Germans, complete and proven men. They were, in short, members of 'an exclusive brotherhood'.

These were the components of the distinctive *esprit de corps* of Hitler's Guard, and to understand this, the very 'life' of the Leibstandarte, is to understand in large part its success during the war. To the usual soldierly attributes of discipline, professionalism, bravery, pride in unit and belief in country, was added a new and potent spirit, the essence of which lay in a unique combination of tough ruthlessness, recklessness in the face of fire which came close to self-sacrifice, and absolute dedication not so much to Hitler as to achievement in battle. It was this which caused the men of the Leibstandarte to behave with such callousness towards their enemies on so many occasions, and at the same time to fight with such bravery against often overwhelming odds.

The Waffen SS was a union of the military and the political. As an SS author expressed it: 'In the past, politics and the armed forces have often pursued divergent paths. The Waffen SS provides the first example of the indissoluble unity of the two, in that concept and sword are welded into one, and political determination brings such strength to the soldier's sword that it renders it invincible.' Thus the Leibstandarte's spirit was not simply of a military nature, for added to it was the political creed of an élite – the National Socialist philosophy expressed in SS terms.

Ideological training, according to the Leibstandarte's chief political education leader, 'is so to influence the Leibstandarte that it can at any time be the shock troops of the régime in ideological struggles . . . to weld the units of the Leibstandarte together and make them into a stout tool in the hands of the Führer'. During the war it was held by some that political indoctrination was of equal importance to combat training since it gave to the often battle-shattered Leibstandarte an all-important spirit and inner cohesion.

The purely political aspects of the Leibstandarte's ethic are not of direct relevance here, suffice it to say that, at first, its members were as imbued as any other National Socialist organization with the theories of 'racial superiority', 'living space', 'Greater Germany' and 'world power'. In his instructions to the SS Panzer Corps in 1943 Himmler stressed the importance of political teaching in the Waffen SS, so that its men 'are really saturated with our spirit . . . We have only one task – to stand firm and carry on the racial struggle without mercy.' The expression that this took in the Leibstandarte was emphatically not that of the concentration camp guards, nor of the security service; rather it was a hardness and contempt for its enemies, an outlook of often total inhumanity which was described by the Reichsführer SS: 'For the SS man there is one absolute principle: he must be honest, decent, loyal and friendly to persons of our own blood – and to no one else.'

To this was added the feeling of outright hatred that was evident in the East, the conflict against the USSR being seen not only as a clash of political systems, as a crusade against Bolshevism, but, more important, as a life-or-death struggle between races. The propaganda to which the fighting SS men were subject was strongly put. One pamphlet described the Slav, against whom the Leibstandarte fought for so long, as a 'subhuman': 'To the outward eye the subhuman is biologically an entirely similar creation of nature [as the human]; he has hands, feet, and a sort of brain, with eyes and a mouth. In fact, however, he is a totally different and frightful creature, a caricature of a man . . . but intellectually and morally lower than any animal. This creature is actuated by a ghastly chaos of savage, unrestrained passions – limitless destructiveness, primitive lust and shameless vulgarity.'

As one historian, J. Gray, has put it: 'When voluntary German SS troopers engaged fanatic Communists . . . a climax of enmity and hatred was reached in which all traces of chivalry vanished and all moderation was abandoned.' Examples abound. One Leibstandarte officer reported that during hand-to-hand fighting the Russians 'beat in the skulls of the wounded with their entrenching tools', and another recalled that some of his men purposely fashioned dum-dum bullets for use against the 'Reds'.

Until mid-1941 the Leibstandarte had an unblemished reputation concerning the treatment of its enemies. Who first began the atrocities on the Eastern Front it is impossible to tell; extermination of prisoners was widespread from the early days of Operation 'Barbarossa'. It soon became the practice to deliver the *coup de grâce* to those wounded who might fall into Soviet hands in order to avoid the possibility of torture. A company commander of the Leibstandarte wrote in August 1941: 'I have never seen such disgusting scenes, whole groups of men from all units have just been murdered by the Soviets upon their surrender . . . It will not last for long.' In April 1942 the Division shot every prisoner taken over a period of three days (some 4,000 men) in retaliation for the murder of six of its members. At Nuremberg the Russians alleged that the Leibstandarte and Totenkopf divisions between them were 'responsible for the extermination of more than 20,000 peaceful citizens of Kharkov, for the shooting and burning alive of prisoners of war'. This attitude of utter ruthlessness was continued in the West. In Italy the town of Boves and its inhabitants were 'destroyed' by the Leibstandarte as part of an anti-guerrilla operation, and in the Ardennes the massacre of seventy-one American prisoners at Malmédy was paralleled by other such incidents, often against civilians. At Stavelot, for example, ninety-three men, women and children were killed by small-arms fire, although how many were actually murdered it is impossible to tell.

However, a Viennese journalist who served with Hitler's Guard in the first Russian campaign was able to describe the very correct behaviour shown by the Leibstandarte towards the Kherson Jews (they were killed by an SS Einsatzgruppe two months later), and told of the sympathetic treatment towards the Russian civilians. Attempts were made to stop indiscriminate shooting of prisoners, Dietrich urging that 'we owe it to the title on our sleeves'. One platoon commander was so incensed at seeing one of his men maliciously wounding a Soviet prisoner that he shot him; another tried no less than three times to court-martial men for killing defenceless Russians, it being 'un-German and prejudicial to discipline'. At the end of the Balkan campaign a unit of the Leibstandarte even went so far as to actively protect the withdrawal of the defeated Greek forces (for whom they had a strong admiration) from pursuit by the vengeful Italians.

While evidence is scanty it does seem probable that many of the atrocities committed were perpetrated not so much through any strongly developed National Socialist ardour or excess of zeal, but rather through the ruthlessness and disregard for human life which, when in action, characterized the Waffen SS.

Every coin has its reverse, and there also existed within the Waffen SS a distinctly anti-SS spirit, to which was added by the end of the war what can only be described as an anti-Hitler feeling. This conflict in attitude which manifested itself in the 'Führer's Own' is on the surface puzzling, but it was perhaps inevitable that it should evolve owing to the military role assumed by the armed SS and to the realities of war with which it was thereby confronted.

From the beginning the élite nature of Hitler's Guard and of the SS-VT tended to set them apart from the rest of the SS. Himmler noticed in 1937 that 'they tend to affect a superior air when in contact with us lesser mortals'. This attitude was fostered by the increasing military duties of the armed SS, its commitment to the field of battle and its resulting close contact with the Wehrmacht, so that by 1943 Himmler found himself forced to write: 'The Waffen SS is reaching such a stage of independence from its political background, that I fear it will lose its identity to the armed forces.' This 'Wehrmacht mentality' found expression through the increasing

use of military ranks (strongly forbidden by the Reichsführer SS), the shunning of contacts with the 'politicals'
and a noticeable improvement of relations with the Army.
Ideological training in the Waffen SS, which was in theory
to be so intense, was in practice often lax, being regarded
in the main as not of direct relevance to its military duties,
so much so that the SS Hauptamt grew most concerned
about it. In February 1943, for example, it issued an
instruction urging the officers to train their soldiers 'to be
more fanatical and convinced standard bearers of the
National Socialist ideology and the concept of our Führer
Adolf Hitler'. But exhortations such as this were of little
avail; the armed SS men continued to grow away from
Himmler's SS Order, to turn in on themselves and to
create their own distinctive spirit – the ideals and the
exclusiveness of a military élite.

At the end, not only did National Socialist ideology
come to be disregarded by many in the Waffen SS, but
some of its soldiers even began to react strongly against
it. In particular a few who fought the Russians questioned
the clearly ridiculous philosophy that they were 'subhuman'.

The contrast between theory and practice is well exem-
plified by a discussion held by SS legal officers who met in
May 1943 to discuss the fact that Waffen SS men were
indulging in sexual relationships with women of other
races, including Slavs (a forbidden practice which ran
counter to National Socialist racial theory). One volun-
teered the information that 'In the Leibstandarte sexual
intercourse with females of other races was very frequent
. . . Some men more or less kept a concubine', and
another lamented that he had been told that the Commander of the Leibstandarte had stated that 'this order
[against intercourse] did not apply to his unit. This order

has been issued by theoretical experts.' The realities of war did not deal kindly with a baseless ideology.

By 1944 the prospect of defeat coupled with the high casualty rates had caused many officers to question Hitler's conduct of the war. One security report spoke of 'a possible, or potential, or even an acute difference of opinion between the Führer and the SS or Waffen SS'. This found its most potent outlet in a group of senior Waffen SS officers, Dietrich included, who were prepared to disobey their Führer and who were even in contact with the German Resistance. It is quite possible that had Rommel been in a position to act against Hitler in late 1944, then Dietrich would have joined him. As it was, he expressed reluctance to any idea of marching upon Paris to restore order after the July Plot, and he took great pains to obtain the release from the security police of General Speidel, one of the conspirators. The estrangement of Dietrich from Hitler continued. Before the Ardennes offensive the former Guard Commander had strong doubts as to its outcome and privately even questioned the sanity of his Führer whose plan it was.

Such acute disillusion, however, was not widespread in Hitler's Guard, and certainly the actions of its members during the battles of 1944 and 1945 reveal little of hesitation or of doubt. It was only at the end of March 1945, when Hitler ordered them to be stripped of their armbands for supposedly failing him in action, that belief in their Führer finally deserted the SS men, and, in the words of one of them, 'left us with nothing but our dead'.

3

Recruitment, Training, Organization and Uniform

Recruitment

'I will have no one in my Leibstandarte who is not of the best Germany can offer.' Such was Hitler's requirement for his Guards, one echoed by a recruiting pamphlet when it asserted that 'the special tasks of the SS compel us to apply the unalterable laws of selection and to recruit only the most valuable men'.

Applicants to join the Leibstandarte had to be between the ages of seventeen and twenty-two, at least 5ft 11in tall (later 6ft 0.5in) and of the highest physical fitness. Himmler insisted that every SS man must be 'of well-proportioned build; for instance there must be no disproportion between the lower leg and the thigh, or between the legs and the body; otherwise an exceptional bodily effort is required to carry out long marches'. It was no idle boast of his that 'until 1936 we did not accept a man in the Leibstandarte . . . if he had even one filled tooth. We were able to assemble the most magnificent manhood in that early Waffen SS.' Recruiting qualifications reflected ideology. Appearance should be truly Nordic, Himmler writing: 'The point is that in his attitude to discipline the man should not behave like an underling, that his gait, his hands, everything should correspond to the ideal which we set ourselves.' His Aryan pedigree, too, had to be spotless. From the end of 1935 every SS man had to be able to produce a record of his ancestry, for other ranks back to 1800, for officers to 1750. If any trace of Jewish or other 'undesirable' blood were

detected, the man was either refused entry or, if it came
to light later, ejected from the SS. Dietrich commented in
disgust that 'some forty good specimens at least are kept
from joining the Leibstandarte every year due to doubt
concerning ancestry'. As a corollary to this, any woman
wishing to marry an SS man had to submit her ancestry
for examination, as well as a photograph of herself in
bathing costume. However, there were exceptions. The
son of a high-ranking SS officer, although he was found
to have 'a full-Jewish ancestor in 1711' on his mother's
side, was nevertheless allowed to join Hitler's Guard.

In peacetime membership of the armed SS was voluntary, and, even when the exigencies of war forced it to
accept numbers of conscripts, this aspect remained
important. As an SS instruction put it: 'A decision to join
the Führer's military force is equally nothing less than the
expression of a voluntary determination to continue the
present political struggle upon another level.' From 1935,
membership of the Leibstandarte and SS-VT counted as
military service, but its terms were hard – a minimum of
four years for enlisted men, twelve for NCOs and twenty-
five for officers. Rates of pay, from August 1938, corre-
sponded to those of the Wehrmacht. Before 1939, a
member of the SS-VT could always obtain his release
from its ranks if he were sufficiently determined so to do
(in 1937, for example, eighty-four men left), but the war
put an end to this.

Although considerable restrictions were placed upon
recruitment to the Waffen SS – for example, before the
war it was not allowed to advertise in the press – the
desire of many young Germans to become members of an
ideological and military élite, coupled with Hitler's
endeavours to keep his Guard up to strength, ensured
that the Leibstandarte, unlike other armed SS units,
would have few manpower problems. However, war

inevitably took its toll both in quality and quantity, and by 1943 the Leibstandarte had been forced to lower its standards. Ethnic Germans from Hungary, Slovakia and Romania, some of whom were in their fifties, were even to be found within its ranks. The last draft received by Hitler's Guard consisted of an assorted collection of personnel from the Luftwaffe, the Navy and the factories, a proportion of whom were above active-service age.

Training

Once in the Waffen SS the aim of the commanders was to create 'a supple, adaptable soldier, athletic of bearing, capable of more than average endurance on the march and in combat'. He was to be 'as much at home on the battlefield as on the athletic field'. After training the SS-VT could cover 3km (1.88 miles) in twenty minutes while in full battle-kit (some 60lb). This was made possible by the great emphasis placed upon physical exercise and sports, which were made an integral and continual part of the training programme and daily life. One enterprising young company commander of the Leibstandarte used to run with his men five miles a day, and, in order to show his contempt for the elements, increased this to seven miles in bad weather. More time was spent in the field, on the ranges, and in the classroom learning the theory of tactics, than was the practice in the Army, while considerably less attention was given to drill. This resulted in a standard of battlefield movement and shooting that was appreciably higher than the average in the Wehrmacht.

Training exercises were made as realistic as possible, the conditions of combat being all too vividly simulated with live ammunition and artillery fire. This, according to Himmler, 'was so that every man became accustomed to his weapons and also to being within fifty–seventy metres of the explosion of his own artillery fire'. The Army criticized the SS-VT for the casualties which inevitably occurred, but although it was considered 'a shame to lose each good German lad . . . every drop of blood in peacetime saved streams of blood in battle'. The end-product of the training was a high standard of soldier, a man who was an 'assault trooper' rather than just an infantryman or tankman; someone who, when acting in concert with his fellows, 'would by blows of lightning rapidity split the enemy into fragments and then destroy the dislocated remnants' [Steiner].

During the war specialized training schools were instituted for the whole of the Waffen SS, such as the SS Artillery School at Glau and the SS Panzer Grenadier School at Keinschlag, thus reflecting the increasing complexity of war as well as the expansion of the armed SS. Those selected to become NCOs went similarly to special training centres such as the SS-und-Waffen Unterführerschüle Lauenburg (which was instituted on 1st November 1940).

It was popularly thought that the Waffen SS suffered from bad officers. One report noted 'voices are to be heard saying that the Waffen SS possesses no trained officers, and that SS men are therefore recklessly sacrificed'. However, this was not the case. At its inception the SS-VT did indeed face the problem of a lack of experienced officers, but, as the historian Reitlinger has correctly asserted, 'the Waffen SS was to develop the most efficient of all the military training systems of the Second World War'.

For officers, the armed SS was indeed a career open to talent, the individual records of many Leibstandarte commanders being proof enough of that. Background and schooling were considered secondary to powers of leadership and military ability. Before 1938, 40 per cent of the SS officer-cadets had only received elementary school education and whereas in the armed forces 49 per cent of the officers were of military families, the proportion was only 5 per cent in the SS-VT. Likewise, in the Army less than 2 per cent were of peasant stock, whereas 90 per cent of SS-VT commanders had been brought up on the land. (This, incidentally, reflects the high proportion of recruits which came from the countryside rather than from the towns – in some parts of Germany as many as a third of the farmers' sons joined the ranks of the armed SS – the same areas which gave the greatest support to the NSDAP.)

Potential officers had to serve two years in the ranks before proceeding to the military academies – the foremost being the Junkerschulen Bad Tölz and Braunschweig. At these institutions a tough, thorough training was given; in Reitlinger's words, 'a cross between the Spartan Hoplites and the Guards' Depot at Caterham', and by the end of 1937 they were able to produce between them some 400 officers a year. There are many stories about the tests of courage that took place, most fallacious (for example, the grenade exploding upon a cadet's helmet – completely impossible!), but there is no doubt that on average the type of officer produced was considerably more aggressive in action than his Wehrmacht counterpart. By 1942 nearly all of the first fifty-four cadets who had passed out of Bad Tölz in 1934 had been killed.

Organization

The organization of the Leibstandarte makes a particularly interesting study, for within ten years it developed from a political guard unit to a military formation; from company strength to divisional status.

The SS Stabswache Berlin was instituted on 17th March 1933, and consisted of one SS Sturm (company) of 120 men. In May it was re-formed as SS Sonderkommando Zossen with two SS Stürme, and was amalgamated in

September with the SS Sonderkommando Jüterbog (of three SS Stürme), the new formation being called SS Leibstandarte 'Adolf Hitler'.

By October 1933, the Leibstandarte consisted of a staff, two SS Sturmbanne (battalions), each of three SS Stürme, and one signals Zug (platoon), and some 800 men. Early in 1934 the unit was retitled SS Standarte 1-Leibstandarte SS 'Adolf Hitler' so as to include it within the numbered series of all SS formations. But Hitler, wishing to keep his Guard apart, cancelled the order.

By the middle of 1934 the various components of the Leibstandarte were known by military terms – i.e. Battalion, Kompanie, etc. – despite strong protests from the Reichsführer SS. By this time, too, a military organization was evolving, each battalion being divided into two rifle companies, a machine-gun company and a signals platoon. A return of strengths on 6th August 1934 revealed that a battalion of Hitler's Guard now consisted of twelve officers, eighty-five NCOs, and 346 men.

With the extension of its duties after June 1934, the Leibstandarte, in common with other armed SS units, was enlarged and organized along military lines. In October the decision was taken to motorize the unit, and at the end of the month the Leibstandarte was composed as follows:

Staff, with signals platoon and Band

I Battalion (divided as above)	13 Company (Motor-cycle)
II Battalion (divided as above)	14 Company (Mortar)
III Battalion (divided as above)	One armoured car platoon

In military terms the Leibstandarte was now a motorized regiment and by 30th May 1935 its total strength had grown to 2,660 men (out of a total SS-VT strength of 8,459 men).

The next four years saw the continued growth of the Leibstandarte. A fourth battalion was instituted to provide guards for the Reich Chancellery and the Berghof, and an infantry-gun company (7.5cm IG), an anti-tank company (3.7cm Pak), a pioneer platoon and a motorcycle platoon were added to the Leibstandarte's battle strength by September 1939. Hitler's Guard now numbered some 3,700 men.

The requirements of war had their effect upon the Leibstandarte, so that by May 1940 it had gained one more infantry-gun company, a light-infantry column and an artillery battalion of three batteries (10.5cm medium field guns). On 6th August 1940 Hitler authorized the expansion of the Leibstandarte to brigade strength, on the 13th its title was slightly altered to Leibstandarte SS 'Adolf Hitler', and on the 19th an artillery regiment, a pioneer battalion, a signals company and a reconnaissance detachment were raised. At the end of the reorganization of the Leibstandarte before the Balkan campaign, its composition was thus:

Headquarters staff with Band

I–III Battalions, each of three rifle, one machine-gun and one heavy company (the heavy company consisted of two anti-tank gun platoons (3.7cm and 5cm Pak) and one each of mortars (8cm) and pioneers)

IV Heavy Battalion of one light infantry-gun company (7.5cm), one heavy infantry-gun company (15cm), one anti-tank gun company (4.7cm self-propelled), one field-gun company (7.5cm self-propelled), and one anti-aircraft gun company (3.7cm)

V Guard Battalion of four companies stationed at Berlin-Lichterfelde

One Reconnaissance Detachment with two motor-cycle companies, one armoured car company (Sd.Kfz 222 and Sd.Kfz 233) and one heavy company

One Artillery Regiment, with one battalion of three batteries (10.5cm), one mixed battalion of three batteries (two of 15cm and one of 8.8cm guns) and one light artillery column

One Pioneer Battalion with three companies, one bridging column and one light pioneer column

One Signals Detachment with one telephone and one wireless
   company
Miscellaneous supply and service units

At the end of the campaign the unit was officially
designated SS Division Leibstandarte 'Adolf Hitler'.

Before the opening of the Russian campaign the Leibstandarte was strengthened by the addition of another
infantry battalion, an anti-aircraft detachment of three
batteries (two of 3.7cm and one of 2cm Flak), one survey
battery, a light signals column, and a field hospital. Its
strength on 30th June 1941 was 10,796 men.

Expansion continued, and on 9th September 1942
Hitler decreed that his Guard should receive the title SS
Panzer Grenadier Division Leibstandarte 'Adolf Hitler'.
Two Panzer Grenadier regiments had been formed out of
the existing infantry battalions in mid-1942, and an
assault-gun detachment (Sturmgeschutz III) and a self-
propelled anti-tank gun detachment (7.5cm Pak 'Marder')
had been created.

In October 1942, the composition of an SS Panzer
Grenadier Regiment was given as:

Headquarters and Band
Escort Company: Motor-cycle Despatch Platoon and Signals
   Platoon
I–III Battalions, each of three companies (of three platoons),
   one machine-gun company, and one heavy company, consist-
   ing of one anti-tank (5cm), one light-infantry gun and one
   pioneer platoon
One Heavy Infantry-Gun Company (Self-Propelled) (15cm
   'Bison')
One Anti-Tank Company (Self-Propelled) (7.5cm)
One Anti-Aircraft Company (Self-Propelled) (2cm)

But of far more significance for the future was the
establishment of a tank battalion (Abteilung) of three
companies as early as 30th January 1942. It was equipped

with Panzers Mk III and IV. In October and November of the same year a tank regiment was formed out of this nucleus – SS Panzer Regiment 1 (two battalions). In December the Leibstandarte received two companies with the new Mk VI Tigers (22 tanks). In the first half of 1943, 100 Mk V Panthers arrived and the Tank Regiment was organized as follows (a paper strength of some 250 tanks):

Headquarters
I Battalion with 1–4 Companies
II Battalion with 5–8 Companies

III Battalion with 8–12 Companies
13 Heavy Company
14 Pioneer Company

In the autumn of 1943, when the Division moved to Italy, the regiment lost its III Battalion.

On 31st December 1942 the strength of the Leibstandarte was 678 officers and 20,166 other ranks (considerably higher than Army divisions), and by the end of 1943 a total of 19,867. On 22nd October 1943 the unit received its final title – I SS Panzer Division Leibstandarte 'Adolf Hitler' (it had been a full Panzer division in all but name for over a year).

Hitler's Guard was now of such a size that it took nearly 150 trains to move the Division minus its armour from the East to Italy.

The Order of Battle of the **Leibstandarte** in March 1944 was:

Divisional headquarters

SS Panzer-Grenadier Regiment No. 1:
  Headquarters
  I Battalion with 1–5 Companies
  II Battalion with 6–10 Companies

III Battalion with 11–15 Companies
16 Anti-aircraft Company
17 Infantry-gun Company
18 Anti-tank Company
19 Reconnaissance Company
20 Pioneer Company

SS Panzer-Grenadier Regiment No. 2:
    Headquarters
    I Battalion with 1–5 Companies
    II Battalion with 6–10 Companies
    III Battalion with 11–14 Companies
    15 Anti-aircraft Company
    16 Infantry-gun Company
    17 Anti-tank Company
    18 Reconnaissance Company
    19 Pioneer Company

SS Panzer-Reconnaissance Detachment No. 1:
    Headquarters
    1–6 Companies

SS Panzer Regiment No. 1:
    Headquarters
    I Battalion with 1–4 Companies
    II Battalion with 5–8 Companies
    Heavy Company
    Pioneer Company

SS Panzer Anti-Tank Detachment No. 1:
    Headquarters
    1–3 Companies

SS Assault-Gun Detachment No. 1:
    Headquarters
    1–3 Companies

SS Panzer Artillery Regiment No. 1:
    Headquarters
    I Battalion with 1–3 Batteries
    II Battalion with 4–6 Batteries
    III Battalion with 7–9 Batteries
    IV Battalion with 10–12 Batteries

SS Anti-Aircraft Detachment No. 1:
    Headquarters
    1–5 Companies
    2cm Flak platoon

SS Panzer Pioneer Battalion No. 1:
    Headquarters
    1–4 Companies

SS Panzer Signals Detachment No. 1:
    Headquarters
    1–2 Companies

On 1st June 1944 the Leibstandarte consisted of 21,386 men, armed with 45 self-propelled guns and 50 Mk IV, 38 Mk V, and 29 Mk VI tanks.

In September 1944 the following unit was added:

SS Mortar Detachment No. 1:
    Headquarters
    1–3 Batteries (15cm)
    4 Battery (21cm)

A return of strengths on 20th September gave nominal numbers of 655 officers, 4,177 NCOs, 14,246 men and 1,029 helpers (20,107).

By mid-December the Leibstandarte had within its battle order 84 tanks and 20 self-propelled guns with the promise of more to come.

For the Ardennes Offensive the Leibstandarte formed **Kampfgruppe (Battle-Group) 'Peiper'** which consisted of:

I Battalion Panzer Regiment
III Battalion Panzer Grenadier Regiment No. 2
II Battalion Artillery Regiment
3 Company Pioneer Battalion
Reconnaissance Detachment
68 Flak Battalion (Luftwaffe)
501 Heavy Panzer Battalion (I SS Panzer Corps) (Tiger IIs)

The I Panzer Battalion was a mixture of the strongest companies of the Regiment, viz:

Headquarters
1 Company (Mk V) } 60 tanks
2 Company (Mk V) }

6 Company (Mk VI) } 60 tanks
7 Company (Mk VI) }
9 Company (Engineers)
Artillery

The Leibstandarte's last battles took enormous toll of its strength at a time when no adequate reinforcements were forthcoming. The situation was so bad that on 7th April 1945 Hitler's Guard was down to a mere 57 officers, 229 NCOs, 1,296 men and 16 tanks in the field.

Just as Hitler ensured that his Guard received large numbers of personnel, so he saw to it that it received generous quantities of the latest and best equipment. As a result the Leibstandarte was organized as one of the strongest six or seven German divisions of the war. In late 1943, for example, the Leibstandarte was sent twenty-two Tiger tanks at a time when Germany's total was only seventy-four.

Order of Battle of the Leibstandarte
September 1939–March 1944

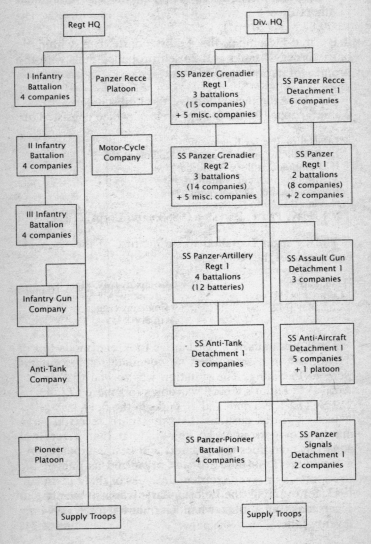

During 1943 and 1944, and upon their introduction into service, the Leibstandarte was equipped with the following:

Assault gun: 15cm Sturmpanzer 'Brummbär'; **Self-propelled guns:** 10.5cm Panzerfeldhaubitze 'Wespe', 15cm Panzerhaubitze 'Hummel'; **Self-propelled anti-tank guns:** 8.8cm 'Nashorn', 7.5cm Jagdpanzer IV, 8.8cm Jagdpanzer Tiger (P) 'Elefant'; **Armoured cars:** Sd.Kfz 234 'Puma' and its variants; **Self-propelled mortar batteries:** 15cm 'Maultier'; as well as a variety of other weapons such as the 2cm four-barrelled Flak 'Wirbelwind' mounted upon standard chassis.

Until mid-1941 the Leibstandarte, as a motorized formation, was equipped with lorries and towing half-tracks (e.g. the Sd.Kfz 10) and to these were added during 1942 armoured personnel carriers – the Sd.Kfz 250, 251 and their variants.

The strengths of the Leibstandarte in both numbers of men and equipment varied greatly during 1939–45 owing to reorganizations, losses and shortages of war. To supplement figures already given, the following give paper strengths for 1944:

A Panzer-Grenadier Company had 34 light machine-guns, 4 heavy machine-guns, 2 8cm mortars, 2 flame-throwers, and 12 Panzerschrecks
A Panzer-Grenadier Machine-gun Company had 12 heavy machine-guns and 6 8cm mortars
An anti-tank gun platoon had 3 guns. (A company had 9)
An infantry-gun platoon had 2 guns. (A company had 6)
An anti-aircraft company had 12 guns
An artillery battery had 4 guns
A mortar detachment had 18 projectors

One source gives the strengths of men in the major components of the Leibstandarte during early 1944 as: Panzer Grenadier Regiments 1 and 2, 3,685 and 3,242 respectively; Panzer Regiment, 2,250; Artillery Regiment, 2,256; and Recce Detachment, 1,104.

The SS Begleitkommando des Führers was the detachment of hand-picked SS men who accompanied the Führer during the war. It consisted mainly of personnel from the Leibstandarte, but also some from the SS Hauptamt and other Waffen SS units. In 1940 this formation came under the command of SS Obersturmführer Franz Schädel.

In January 1940 Hitler ordered that a V Guard battalion be permanently quartered in Berlin, personnel rotating between it and units at the front. In February 1942 the battalion was sent to the Leningrad area to fight as part of an SS Battle Group. In mid-June it joined the Division at the front. At home its place was taken by the skeleton 'Guard Battalion Berlin' at the end of 1942, the latter being replaced by the 'SS Guard Battalion I Berlin' in December 1943.

In mid-1943 the Leibstandarte was required to provide officers and NCOs (possibly as many as 1,000 men) to form and train the new 12 SS Division 'Hitler Jugend'. A little later the I SS Panzer Corps 'Leibstandarte' command was instituted, staffed largely by Leibstandarte personnel (it should not be confused with the Division).

Uniform

Before the war, for ceremonial, guard duties and 'walking-out', the black SS uniform with silver-coloured insignia was the standard dress of the Leibstandarte. It had developed from the simple cap and tie worn by the early SS into an elaborate attire which adequately suited the 'order of knighthood' that Himmler felt his SS to be. It was at once both attractive and sinister, bearing all types of distinctions which immediately set its wearer apart from the plebeian masses. The death's-head badge worn upon the cap was symbolic of the SS spirit – loyal unto death – while the SS runes shown by the armed SS on the right collar denoted the lightning flashes of victory as well as standing for Schutz Staffel (they were only carried by the armed SS).

However, for everyday and military use the black uniform, though imposing, soon proved itself totally inadequate and therefore, by June 1935, the entire Leibstandarte had been issued with an earth-grey service dress. This in its turn began to be replaced in 1937 by a field-grey uniform similar to that worn by the Army – an indication of the future role the SS-VT was to play. In 1938 it was decided that the final form of service uniform for the armed SS was to be army dress, supply being continued until the end of the war (until 1940 the jackets were tailored with dark green collars).

The SS camouflage combat clothing was the most original of all uniform innovations of the period, and has had considerable influence upon post-war military dress. First introduced in 1938, the smock and helmet-cover were used sparingly in the Polish and French campaigns, and then mostly by the assault troops, but camouflage items became extremely widespread later. Worn over the service dress, they provided the easiest way of identifying the Waffen SS in the field (although a few Wehrmacht units also wore camouflage clothing from the end of 1942). There was a wide variety of camouflage designs, and until 1943 the items were made with material that was reversible – one side predominantly green for summer wear, the other in warm brown shades for the rest of the seasons. In 1944 a camouflage uniform – a combined summer-field service and working dress – was introduced. There were a number of other types of camouflage items such as white smocks, complete uniforms made out of Italian material and special dress issued to armoured units.

In common with the Army, soldiers of the Waffen SS

armoured units wore special clothing designed for ease of movement within the confines of tanks and armoured cars. In 1938 a black uniform was introduced (the colour chosen so that grease and dirt would not show up), and in 1941 a field-grey uniform of identical cut was issued to crews of assault guns and, later, to self-propelled anti-tank units.

Other clothing worn by the men of the Leibstandarte included white summer tunics and heavy winter parkas. By the end of the war uniformity of dress, which had never been a strong point of the Waffen SS, was a lost cause, any number of variations being in use – owing in the main to the shortages of material and to the profusion of items introduced over the years.

As part of the armed SS, Hitler's Guard wore SS insignia, but its members were usually readily distinguishable from other SS men. The marks of the Leibstandarte (all silver-grey or silver-coloured) are described in the following list:

a) Most important of all was the armband, 28mm wide, made of black tape with the inscription 'Adolf Hitler' in German script, and worn around the top of the left cuff. (During the war Dietrich had his cuff-title woven in gilt.)

b) The LAH monogram carried on the shoulder straps. After 1943 the Leibstandarte was the only Waffen SS unit allowed to wear such insignia.

c) Before May 1940 the Leibstandarte was the only SS-VT unit to have plain SS runes with no accompanying insignia on the collar-patch.

d) As from 1936 the Leibstandarte was the only unit to carry white equipment on ceremonial occasions.

In addition, the following distinctive SS insignia were worn:

1) The SS version of the National Emblem (the eagle) worn on the cap and on the left upper sleeve.

2) The SS collar-patches (rank insignia being worn on the left for ranks up to and including SS Obersturmbannführer; on both sides for more senior officers).

3) The SS helmet transfers.

4) The death's head worn on the cap.

Military Operations – Leibstandarte SS 'Adolf Hitler'

The Invasion of Poland

Throughout the uneasy summer of 1939 the German Army lay like a sickle around the frontiers of Poland and Hitler's decision to go to war set into motion a campaign which was to fling fifty-five divisions, including every German armoured, motorized and light division, across the great Polish land bridge, a mostly open, rolling country suitable for fast, tank movement and without many natural defence lines.

When on 30th August the German High Command knew that war was inevitable it sent out the code-words which set D-Day as 1st September and H-Hour as 04.45 hours. As the clocks ticked away the last hours of peace the German divisions marched towards their assembly areas under the light of a waning moon. Long columns of guns, vehicles and men went forward, joining with other columns until the whole force formed a river of military might flowing towards Poland. As the units which were to form the first assault wave drew near the frontier, vehicle headlights were extinguished, smoking was forbidden and the formations melted into the dark forests which enclosed the concentration and assembly areas. The assault detachments which had been holding the ground closed up to the frontier wire and moved to their jumping-off points.

The German Army had taken up its battle positions and lay waiting for the dawn, not with any general sense of elation at the thought of the coming war but rather with a determination and firm resolve to do its duty. 'I am writing this by very poor light . . . Today we shall be at war with Poland unless the Poles see sense. Tomorrow I shall be a complete soldier. Personal thoughts I have expelled from my mind; only one single thought remains – Germany.'

The Polish Army, thirty-two divisions strong, which went into the field was inferior to the German Army both qualitatively and quantitatively. The German Army enjoyed a superiority in infantry of 2.3:1; of 4.3:1 in artillery and in armour of 8.2:1, for in the latter case the Poles had only nine companies of 8-ton tanks and twenty-nine companies of armoured weapons carriers. Although both armies used horse-drawn transport and guns the Polish reliance was almost absolute, 92 per cent of all military wheeled transport being horse-drawn.

Polish strategic, defensive planning accepted that the Army would have to give ground and it was further accepted that this sacrifice would entail the loss of the most highly populated and industrial western half of the country. This formed a huge salient into Germany and the Polish armies committed to its defence were outflanked. From north and south two huge German Army Groups were to strike in a three-stage operation. Firstly, the Polish Field Army was to be encircled in a double envelopment east and west of Warsaw. It would then be held and destroyed in a killing ground in the bend of the Vistula. The third stage would be the capture of the Polish capital and of the fortress areas.

The Leibstandarte formed part of Army Group South. Although nominally an independent, motorized regiment it was under the control of 17th Infantry Division on the right flank of Eighth Army. The position of the Leibstandarte in the battle line was determined when von Rundstedt, the Army Group Commander, demanded extra reconnaissance strength for his Tenth Army's left wing. The SS unit was inserted into the line for this purpose and to act as a link between the Eighth and Tenth Armies. Its first tasks approaching from the vicinity of Breslau were to penetrate the fortified frontier line and to capture an important height behind the Prosna river. The Polish troops holding the immediate forward area were part of a regimental infantry and artillery group, a type of outpost unit that was held in front of the main body of each Polish division in the line.

At 04.45 hours hostilities duly commenced and the Eighth Army, with the advantage of surprise, fought its way forward with such *élan* that advances of between three and four miles had been achieved within seventy-five minutes of the frontier being crossed. The initial confusion that ensues whenever troops are committed to battle for the first time was soon overcome and movement forward was continuous. Behind the cushion of frontier detachments the Polish 10th Infantry Division facing the Leibstandarte stood fast in their prepared positions and resisted strongly with 37mm anti-tank guns. The river was crossed by the SS troops; the frontier positions were penetrated and then the lorries drove up through the thinning mist carrying the battalion which was to make an infantry assault upon the heights. With the fluency that intensive training brings the rifle companies debussed and moved forward behind a covering barrage, putting into practice those lessons of fire discipline and tactics which had been learnt on the barrack square at Lichterfelde and on manoeuvres all over Germany. Neither Polish fortifications nor Polish defensive fire nor the difficulties of terrain could halt the advance of those young, volunteer soldiers. The first mission went like clockwork, the assault progressing by bounds, the companies as they deployed being covered by the fire of their comrades. The tactics of fire and movement proved irresistible and the Poles were swept in disorder from the crest.

Some three and a half miles north-westward lay the next objective, the town of Bolestawice. The advance was contested so bitterly by elements of 30th Infantry Division, 21st Infantry Regiment and armoured cars of the Wotyńska Cavalry Brigade that in some sectors no movement forward was possible and those SS units which smashed their way into the Polish lines found that they were under fire from all sides of a salient. Hand-to-hand fighting took place when the Poles counter-attacked with the bayonet. '. . . They came into the attack in long lines, not quite shoulder to shoulder but very close together. They had a battle cry – a long drawn out hurra and we could also hear the officers shouting . . . H . . . says it was "Forward, forward" . . .' The Poles accepted severe losses to halt the advance but the pressure was too strong and by 10.00 hours the town had passed into German hands. Individual prisoners, then groups and finally a steady stream of khaki – green-uniformed men, the Eagle of Poland shining in the welt of their field caps, moved down the road along which the Leibstandarte had attacked.

But the day's objectives had still not all been attained and the Leibstandarte was moved towards the town of Wieruszów, about seven miles away. One column headed along a dirt road leading out of the eastern edge of the town. A central column advanced along the river and the third went via Opatów, struggling through dense birch forests to sever the road west of the town. The countryside was ideal for defence and was held by determined troops who used every scrap of cover; every bush sheltered its small group of Poles, many armed with machine-guns. The long columns of Leibstandarte vehicles were frequently halted as dismounted attacks were made upon nests of resistance. It was, therefore, not until evening that Wieruszów was reached and the position secured for the night. The Leibstandarte took stock of the day's successes. All the objectives had been taken; the 10th, 17th and 25th Polish Infantry Divisions had been identified and prisoners taken from these and from the Wielkopolska and Wotyńska Cavalry Brigades.

The SS unit now moved forward of the main body of the Army to take up its allotted role of flank guard. During the following night reorganization took place at battalion and regimental level, but each company nevertheless spent the night in patrolling aggressively and in beating off cavalry attacks. A dawn 'stand-to' was not necessary. The SS stood to arms all night.

At 06.00 hours on the morning of 2nd September, the men and vehicles of the Leibstandarte were on their way. The unusually dry weather had lowered the level of the rivers and the Prosna offered no obstacle as the main body of the Eighth Army streamed across it heading for the Warta river, a primary defence line, strongly fortified with pill-boxes.

The German strategic plan was yielding results; Tenth Army had begun to break through north of Częstochowa and on 3rd September units from two Panzer divisions, exploiting a gap between the Lódź and Kraków armies, stormed across the Pilica river and headed north-eastward towards Warsaw. The jaws of the German pincers were beginning to close around the armies west of the capital. The Polish High Command ordered a withdrawal to a deep defence line based on Szczerców–Lenkawa. This compression of the Polish western army groups was, unknown to either combatant, the beginning of the end of the campaign, for the Poles were withdrawing into a long, narrow pocket within which they were eventually to be contained, isolated and then destroyed. But the Germans were not to achieve this destruction for another fortnight and during those fourteen days there were to be periods of acute crisis for them at all levels of command from battalion up to that of army group.

The first of these crises came during 4th September when Army Group South realized that between the Warta and the Bzura rivers there was a mass of seven Polish divisions withdrawing in front of Army Group North. As soon as it became aware of the threat to its flank Army Group South changed front to face the force which was thrusting south-eastwards. A frontal assault upon Lódź was ordered for Eighth Army, which was to contain the pressure upon its northern flank while the centre and right wings would smash the Poles at the approaches to Lódź.

The Leibstandarte, meanwhile, was involved in fighting its way towards the small market town of Pabianice, a road and railway junction on the river Ner and a strongpoint in the secondary defence line. The town was held by a garrison whose artillery strength had been bolstered by heavy anti-tank guns and whose morale was high. For three days the Leibstandarte fought its way forward through the outer defence lines guarding the Lódź region. All the SS battalions were committed to battle but could only advance with difficulty against forces which had now been reinforced by 2nd Kaniow Rifle Regiment as well as by a number of *ad hoc* units. The SS advance was contested not least by Polish riflemen, trained woodsmen who combined the huntsman's skills of marksmanship and the use of ground. Well camouflaged and often hidden in positions set high in trees these snipers waited, watched and then struck at selected targets. Single motor-cycle despatch riders or staff cars travelling without escort were favourite targets. The SS defence tactic against these

Polish sharp-shooters was to bombard suspected trees and bushes with a rain of rifle grenades.

The determined resistance put up by the Poles turned the battle into a slogging match fought under hot and cloudless skies. This part of Poland was cultivated with large areas of sunflowers or maize and in these vast fields small and bitter battles were fought with small groups, even individuals, stalking each other through the tall plants. In carefully concealed hides the Poles would hold their fire until the SS men were at point-blank range. A quick burst, a hand grenade and then the Poles would vanish. The SS took to wearing their camouflaged jackets and helmet covers, finding that these blended well with the green shade beneath the sunflower heads. They also adopted the patient tactic of letting the enemy come on and soon had the Poles beaten at their own game.

'The Poles are devilish cunning . . . We had a mission yesterday and had to clear a group of them from a field of maize. We thought they were a handful of stragglers and that a quick sweep would finish our mission . . . They had dug-outs with crops growing on the roof and were almost invisible and hard to detect. We [next line partially illegible] and had to stalk them like characters from a Karl May Wild West novel. When we found a dug-out we blew it up with bundles of grenades. Some of them [dug-outs] may have been linked by tunnels; a combat report had mentioned this . . . We captured more than fifty and it took us hours before we had wiped out this nest . . .'

Late in the evening of 6th September battle orders for the following day made Pabianice the main objective and ordered that Łódź be sealed off from the south-east along the Ragów–Wola Rakowa heights. The first assault, against the western edge of the town, went in during the forenoon of the 17th and was carried out by 23rd Panzer Regiment, but faced by heavy and well-directed fire the tanks could make no progress. The Polish defence tactic was to fire two shots in rapid succession against a small area of the German armoured vehicles and the Polish guns were indeed able to penetrate the lightly armoured Mark I and II tanks at quite long distances. At close range even the more heavily armoured Mark III and IV types could be knocked out by the Polish double punch. With a number of machines thus destroyed at the outset the divisional commander ordered the Panzers to be withdrawn and for the SS infantry to be sent in. The 1st and 2nd Companies of the Leibstandarte then moved forward across the start-line past the tanks withdrawing under heavy fire. The intensity of the SS peacetime training coupled with battle experience had made the men of the Leibstandarte proficient in set-piece attacks and even before they had crossed the start-line the squads had shaken down into tactical formation.

Maximum support was to be given to the assault on Pabianice and artillery officers were sent up with the leading elements so that observed fire could be brought down immediately upon selected targets. Mortars joined in the bombardment. The infantry attack began to roll. The pace of the SS advance carried it through the first line of Polish resistance towards the centre of the town. Automatic weapons, field guns, even anti-tank guns were used in an attempt to halt them. A Polish counter-attack was met in the open street and tumbled into ruin. But the advance of the units flanking the Leibstandarte had not kept equal pace and the SS point group formed a salient which was under fire from all sides. The need to drop off small sections of men to hold the walls of the salient, together with the casualties which had been suffered, had so reduced the power of the SS attack that it began to run out of steam. The Poles suffered no such shortage of men as units withdrawing from the west arrived they were put straight into battle. The western wall of the salient began to give under pressure and so the SS could not consolidate their slender hold on the town, for immediately the Poles launched more counter-attacks. Their infantry and cavalry came charging in every sort of assault formation. These attacks forced the Leibstandarte on to the defensive and then began to force it back, down the streets through which it had advanced, back to the houses on the edge of town. Polish troops debouching from the centre of Pabianice sneaked their way forward, sniping at the HQ personnel and often advancing close enough to them to throw grenades. Heavy pressure was building up. A Polish drive, led with great determination and carried out despite severe losses, brought the Poles up to and then into the field in which the Leibstandarte HQ was located. The Headquarters Defence Platoon was already in action so cooks and drivers were put into the line. At times the Polish onslaught threatened to overrun the Regimental Command Group and to cut the life-line between HQ and the troops but the Leibstandarte defence stood firm.

Fighting conducted at such a level of intensity cannot be of long duration and the Polish effort died away. Both sides broke off the battle to carry out the urgent tasks of regrouping and reinforcement. In this respect the German organization was superior and enabled the SS to be ready to meet the climax of that terrible day. At about 14.30 hours the Poles came on again. Whipped to a frenzy they charged in one final, despairing effort, the infantry line coming forward with a determination to win or to die. 'Through the trodden-down vegetation they stormed; across the bodies of their fallen comrades. They did not come forward with their heads bowed like men in heavy rain – and mostly storming infantry come on like that – but they came with their heads held high like as if they were swimmers breasting the waves. They didn't falter

. . .' Without wavering, the lines of Polish soldiers followed each other through the German fire, but there comes a time when even the bravest fail and the attack was crushed under the heavy barrage of shells and bullets. Some individual soldiers continued to advance alone when all around them had fallen and they carried on charging until they too collapsed in the hurricane of fire.

With the failure of this Polish assault the heart went out of the Pabianice garrison and the prisoners began to come in tens, then in twenties and then in hundreds. The situation which had looked critical for the Leibstandarte in the forenoon had been restored, although the effort which the SS troops had made had so mixed up their companies that no advance upon the town could be resumed until evening.

Pressure by Army Group South compelled a further withdrawal by the Poles, the execution of which left a gap at Petrów and through this breach German tank columns roared up the best road in Poland. The race for the Polish capital was on but the advance needed more motorized infantry support. The Leibstandarte was thereupon detached from Eighth Army and posted to Tenth Army's 4th Panzer Division, whose advanced elements had reached Ochota, a suburb of Warsaw, at 17.15 hours on 8th September.

A battle group made up of the Leibstandarte, the 33rd Infantry Regiment and ancillary services was given the task of cutting the Grodzisk–Masczowoc road, south-east of Warsaw, to prevent the Poles escaping from the pocket in which they were trapped. Breakout attempts by General Knoll's 14th, 17th, and 25th Polish Divisions protected by two cavalry brigades had struck towards Lódź and this movement was to be held and the Poles forced to withdraw to the selected killing ground.

Fresh orders then directed 1st Battalion of the Leibstandarte to move on Oltarzew, a town on the Warsaw road, while the other two battalions took up positions to capture Btonie, east of 1st Battalion and also on the road to the Polish capital. The 1st Battalion arrived in position and immediately came under attack, for the Poles were fighting to keep the road open, the life-line of the Pomorze Army. Regardless of losses the Poles hurled themselves at the SS positions. At first the battalion had only light weapons to counter the assault but soon the artillery component had arrived, unlimbered and had gone into action. Polish columns were halted under the murderous fire; some drivers more adventurous or more desperate than others tried to force their vehicles through the blocked traffic only to make the situation worse. Soon the Polish columns were inextricably entangled. Troops of horse artillery stormed out of the smoke and mist of the evening and rode into point-blank fire, only to be cut down. All through that long night of horror the German guns bombarded the columns lying immobile and confused along the arrow-straight road. The dawn light showed that not only soldiers but also civilians, refugees and others who had been withdrawing under the protection of the Polish Army had fallen victim to the artillery fire. The dead – civilians and military – cattle and horses lay in heaps in the ditches and in the clearings along the road.

The exhausted 1st Battalion was relieved but the 2nd and 3rd Battalions were still fighting hard for the important road and rail junction of Btonie.

From 10th September and for the following two days the encircled Polish armies attacked towards Lódź but they could make no headway and changed the direction of their assault. These new attacks, led by armoured fighting vehicles and armoured cars, struck particularly heavily against the battle group consisting of the Leibstandarte, the 2nd Battalion of 33rd Regiment and the 2nd Battalion of the 4th Panzer Artillery Regiment. But now the Army Group, having contained the Poles in its sector, began to move in to destroy them. The 4th Panzer Division closed up towards the Bzura river, pushing 28th and 30th Polish Divisions towards Modlin. Between the Polish forces on the Bzura and in the Warsaw area there was now a solid mass of German armour. The Polish pocket was isolated. Although it was clear that Polish resistance in some areas was slackening, courage remained high in others. At Glowko the Wielkopolska Cavalry, reduced in numbers by ten days' fighting, continued to attack with determination until it was almost completely destroyed and 30th Division was still fighting hard in the Radziwill forest. During the evening of 12th September the Polish breakout attempt by 4th and 16th Infantry Divisions was driven back with heavy loss. The German ring was absolutely solid.

On the following day the Leibstandarte supported by tanks attacked towards the high ground west of Btonie. The Panzer Regiment formed two columns each supported by a battalion of SS. The lightning attack began. Kaputy was stormed and the armoured thrust continued at top speed, for the order was that there would be no halt. Before dark the objective had been taken and the line consolidated at Leszno and at Bislutki. Throughout the succeeding days the bitter fighting continued. At Sochaczew the battle was particularly fierce and Polish records show that the last commander of Sochaczew was a private soldier, all the officers and NCOs having fallen in combat.

The reduction of the Polish divisions continued during 16th September when 35th Panzer Regiment, the 12th Rifle Regiment and the Leibstandarte made a lorry-borne assault across the Bzura. At the river engineers were working frantically constructing a bridge but there was no time to wait for this to be completed. The armoured vehicles drove headlong down the steep, eastern bank into the water and began to cross the wide, shallow river. Behind the lower, western bank each house was a Polish strongpoint, every patch of undergrowth a defensive position. As the Panzers breasted the western bank a storm of artillery crashed down upon them.

After more than a fortnight of fine, dry, 'Hitler' weather, rain had now begun to fall and this so muddied the exits from the Bzura that the vehicles were unable to manoeuvre. Fording the river had not proved to be such a quick method of passage and the tanks reaching the western bank were too few in number to effect a break-out. The attack was postponed until 11.00 hours by which time sufficient armour had been concentrated. When the attack was finally under way it was, initially, a single armoured fist, striking at the Polish positions, but at Bijampol the column divided to become a pincer movement. The northern arm reached the Mtodzieszyn–Russki road and brought the fleeing Polish troops under bombardment, but at Adamowa the southern arm of the pincer was driven back by anti-tank guns, skilfully hidden and firing at point-blank range. General Kutrzeba, commanding the Pomorze Army, was using his artillery to hammer a corridor through to Warsaw. The German and the Polish assaults had met head on and the outnumbered German column stood in the path of the main Polish thrust. Waves of infantry came in behind the barrage driving back the Leibstandarte battalion. A withdrawal was ordered and the squadrons retired in the drizzle of late afternoon until the whole of 1st Panzer Battalion and the SS was back in the divisional laager. The 2nd Panzer Battalion could not disengage itself from the enemy and spent the whole night fighting off heavy and continuous attacks.

The SS renewed the attack on 17th September but throughout that day and the next there were only minor clashes with the Poles. Late on the night of the 18th came the news that across the Bzura part of 36th Panzer Regiment and 1st SS Battalion was in danger of being overrun. This German attack had also struck a Polish breakout attempt and the mass of 4th Panzer Division, taken in flank, was fighting without any central command. Ammunition and petrol were both running short.

The 35th Panzer Regiment and the two remaining battalions of the Leibstandarte mounted a rescue operation on 19th September. Wherever opposition was met it was removed with such precision that within an hour of the attack moving off the SS and the Panzer men had broken through the Polish ring and linked up. This affair marked both an end and a beginning. The end was that of Polish hopes. However fierce their attacks, however tenacious their defence, it was clear that these were the throes of a dying army. The beginning was of a general advance along the Vistula towards Wysgorod and the destruction of the Polish pocket. At Sladow the 2nd Panzer Battalion, with its SS component, halted to form a front facing east.

The Polish Army was disintegrating under the ceaseless artillery and Luftwaffe bombardment and the final battles in the pocket were fought for possession of the Vistula road connecting Modlin with Warsaw. 'Our advance took us across that part of the battlefield which had been held by the so-called Pomorze Army. The whole area was a scene of death and destruction. The bloated bodies of men and animals blackening under the hot sun, smashed carts, burnt-out vehicles and those most tragic victims of war, the wounded horses, waiting for the mercy shot.

Everywhere there was evidence of a beaten army covering the ground. Now I understand what the words of our song mean: "Man and horse and waggon, the Lord God struck them all down" . . .'

The most successful and destructive encirclement in military history, up to that date, had been concluded and the Polish Army had been destroyed in the bend of the Bzura river. The first and second stages of the High Command plan were over. Now the third stage could be put into operation: the capture of Warsaw and of the key fortress areas. For many of the German troops the fighting along the Bzura river marked the end of their part in the campaign but this was not true of the Leibstandarte which was moved towards Modlin, a fortress area guarding the approach to Warsaw from the north. The Polish garrison was withdrawn into Forts I, II, and III and massed German artillery began a systematic destruction of these works, aided by dive bombers of 4 Air Fleet.

Warsaw held out until 27th September, but with its surrender the Germans were free to concentrate all their forces to attack Modlin. At 07.30 hours on the 28th, General Thomme surrendered the forts. The rain for which the Poles had been praying for nearly a month then began to fall in a drenching downpour, but the campaign was over.

On 25th September, Adolf Hitler visited detachments of the Leibstandarte and inspected No. 13 Company in encampment near Guzow. With the end of the campaign Hitler's Guard was ordered to move, not to the Western Front, as many had anticipated, but to Prague. In that city the Leibstandarte was accorded a rapturous reception and given leave, but the period of rest soon passed and the SS soldiers retrained and refitted for the battles which lay ahead.

Holland and France: Code-word 'Danzig'

All through the long and bitter winter of 1939–40, the Leibstandarte trained for the battles which would be fought in the West. Hitler, who visited the Regiment in winter quarters during December, forecast that they would soon be fighting in regions on which their fathers' blood had been shed, but gave no more precise details. Training, however, laid stress on fast movement and the rapid seizure of bridges. During February operational orders located the Leibstandarte in Eighteenth Army. The role of the Eighteenth Army as part of von Bock's Army Group B was to protect the northern flank of the German Army during the forthcoming Western campaign. The task of the 227th Infantry Division under whose command the Leibstandarte was placed was to break through the Dutch frontier and to capture, intact, the river and road bridges on the axis of advance to the Ijssel river.

On 9th May 1940, code-word 'DANZIG' was flashed to all units of the Wehrmacht, the signal which set in motion the advance to the English Channel. Shortly after midnight the battalions of the Leibstandarte moved out of their Rhineland billets, speeded on their way by the good luck wishes of the local population. At the Dutch frontier the final details were completed and at 05.30 hours, on 10th May, as dawn brought on the new day, a small detachment of the SS captured the bridge at De Poppe and thus opened the road for the waiting columns.

The new opponent of the Leibstandarte, the Royal Dutch Army, had been so long at peace that it was in a run-down condition. Only four Army corps, each of two divisions, formed the bulk of the available forces. To these were added a light division, mounted on bicycles and motor-cycles, a number of infantry brigades, frontier battalions, a regiment of Hussars and fourteen regiments of Army artillery.

The principal Dutch weakness lay in its artillery, composed as it was of mainly obsolete and obsolescent equipment. This weakness was particularly acute in the anti-tank and anti-aircraft arms. With weak and underarmed forces the Dutch faced the dual problems of long frontiers and an almost indefensible terrain. The military solution was to delay the enemy advance, firstly along the frontier; then along the Ijssel–Maas river line and then to hold out along a so-called Valley line, extending from the Zuider Zee southwards to the Maas. This main defensive position was to be manned by 4th, 7th, 8th and 2nd Divisions.

Although this plan appreciated that much Dutch territory in the north and east of the country would fall, quickly, into the hands of an invading enemy the speed at which the Germans moved during the campaign was to prove a complete surprise to the Dutch.

The Leibstandarte, forming the right, i.e. northern flank of the 227th Infantry Division, was able to make a swift advance from the De Poppe bridge on the well-maintained roads and with almost no opposition from any of the five, frontier battalions defending the area. Road blocks were unmanned and such demolitions as had been carried out were so ineffective that they were of nothing more than nuisance value. The first, serious check did not occur until Bornbroek, where the canal bridge was blown, but the SS, using barn doors as improvised rafts, crossed the waterway under fire and rapidly established a bridgehead. The first motor-cycles were ferried across and patrols were sent out to prevent the destruction of other bridges on the line of advance. Back at the canal the SS Pioneers were busy erecting a light bridge but the men of the Anti-tank gun Company, unwilling to wait for this to

be completed, were bringing their pieces across using
human muscle as the motive power.

Shortly before midday the advance guard captured
Zwolle where streets full of civilians and unprepared
soldiers showed clearly that the German arrival was
completely unexpected. This was not surprising for the
Leibstandarte had advanced nearly fifty miles in six hours.
Having accepted the surrender of Zwolle the Regiment
was redeployed south to the main body of the Division
and during this move one of the point sections captured a
Dutch unit at lunch.

On 11th May, the 227th Division was concentrated into
three strike columns. The 1st and 2nd Battalions of the
Leibstandarte formed the right flank. The 3rd SS Battalion, supported by a battalion from 366th Infantry
Regiment, made up the centre while the remainder of
366th and 402nd Infantry Regiments composed the
southern column. The assault was delayed by the destruction of two bridges across the Ijssel but 3rd Battalion
forced a crossing of the river at Zutphen and took Hoven,
on the north–south main railway line, by 14.00 hours,
thus completing the capture of all the day's objectives.
During the fighting SS Obersturmführer Kraas led a deep
penetration across the Ijssel and for more than forty miles
into enemy territory, capturing more than a hundred
Dutch soldiers. For this singular act he was awarded the
Iron Cross, First Class; the first officer to win this decora-
tion during the campaign.

The Leibstandarte was then posted from the 227th to
the 9th Panzer Division and moved via Kleve and Herto-
genbusch to come into the line as a follow-up unit to that
division's northern column. Brushing aside the light
Dutch opposition the SS column went up with the Panzers
during the afternoon of the 13th May. At 04.00 hours
next morning the Leibstandarte supported 9th Panzer

Division's thrust towards the three-quarter-mile-long Maas bridge at Moerdijk, with the task of relieving the paratroops who had captured it, then to enter Rotterdam from the south-east and to seize, by *coup de main*, the Government in The Hague. The advance was made, under intermittent Dutch artillery fire, along the south bank of the Maas, and across the front of the Dutch Light and 5th Infantry Divisions which were holding the line from Rotterdam to Rossum.

By 14th May, having delayed the advance of Eighteenth Army, the Dutch armies lay behind the main defence line, but they were completely cut off from their allies and had no expectation of military help from either France or Great Britain. But the Dutch resistance was obstructing the German High Command plan and an ultimatum was issued that unless this opposition ceased Rotterdam and Utrecht would be destroyed by air and artillery bombardments. The Dutch acceptance of the demand made the German action unnecessary and orders were issued cancelling the artillery bombardment but, as a result of a tragic misunderstanding, the Luftwaffe was let loose upon Rotterdam. After the bombing had ended the SS Reconnaissance Detachment moved into the blazing city to effect a link-up with the parachute unit which had landed during the first day's operations and had subsequently been cut off. The road forward showed how severe had been the fighting. Crashed and burnt-out aeroplanes, many of them Ju 52s, were scattered across the fields and along the highways. In some sectors Dutch resistance, put up by troops who had obviously not received the surrender order, was still strong and had to be subdued. One incident during this confused period resulted in the wounding of the German paratroop General Student. He was arranging with the local Dutch commander the disarming of the forces in the area when the Leibstandarte advance guard roared up in its drive northwards to The Hague. What the SS men saw were hundreds of armed enemy soldiers upon whom they immediately opened fire. One shot hit General Student who fell bleeding from a head wound and this unfortunate accident marred the successful operations which the Leibstandarte had carried out.

The campaign in the Netherlands was nearly over. The German strategy, although delayed, was not out of joint and the bulk of Eighteenth Army, leaving only a mopping-up force, could now be deployed south to support the break-through operations now in motion in northern France. The High Command strategy for the campaign in the West had achieved the first of its intentions: the securing of the right flank. The stage had now been set for the second phase: the separation of the British and French armies, leading up to phase three, the individual destruction of those forces.

By 24th May, the Leibstandarte, now under command of 1st Panzer Division, part of Kleist's Group, began to arrive in position on the line of the Aa Canal, along the southern and eastern side of the evacuation perimeter at Dunkirk into which British and French forces had been compressed.

Although the Regiment had had a long and tiring night march, the 3rd Battalion was ordered to capture the 140ft-high hill, the Wattenberg, which lies to the east of the Aa Canal and which dominates the otherwise flat countryside. Shortly before the attack was due to roll an order from Hitler's headquarters forbade any movement across the canal towards Dunkirk. In defiance of those orders, the regimental commander, 'Sepp' Dietrich, sent his men in. Under the protection of a heavy artillery barrage No. 10 Company crossed the canal and fought its way into Watten. Allied counter-attacks several times threatened to drive the SS out of the town but the mass of 3rd Battalion swept through the point company, smashed the Anglo-French defence, captured the hill and consolidated the position.

Guderian, the Panzer commander, then ordered an attack towards the Wormhoudt–Berques road. For this operation the Leibstandarte, under command of 20th (Motorized) Infantry Division, had 76th Infantry Regiment on its right flank and the 'Grossdeutschland' Regiment on its left. German accounts of the battle describe an Allied infantry spoiling attack launched on 27th May, from a copse east of the Wattenberg, but this is clearly a reference to an attempt by Bren gun carriers and anti-tank guns of British 144th Brigade to seal off the German break-out at Watten. At 08.20 hours the Leibstandarte's 1st Battalion finally got its attack under way but met fierce opposition at Bollezelle. Although the SS unit was forming a salient and was under fire from the rear, left flank, a sector which the 'Grossdeutschland' Regiment should have captured, it was felt that British resistance was weakening and the pressure was maintained until the objective had been taken. On the following day a combined armoured and infantry force made up of the Leibstandarte, 2nd Panzer Brigade and 11th Rifle Brigade attacked Wormhoudt. The SS made a determined assault through a strong defensive barrage laid down by the British artillery, pressing home the attack with great vigour.

During that day, at Esquelberg, while on a journey to co-ordinate the attacks of his battalions, 'Sepp' Dietrich was cut off. His car was fired on and set alight by men of 5th Battalion the Gloucestershire Regiment, belonging to 48th Division, and Dietrich together with his adjutant had to hide in a ditch to wait for their men to rescue them. Attacks by Nos. 2 and 15 Companies failed to reach the

SS commander, nor was an attempt using armoured vehicles of the Tank Brigade's No. 6 Company any more successful. The British defence of Esquelberg was the most severe opposition that the SS had encountered and this resistance was thought by the Germans to be maintained by first-class, élite troops. In fact the men who were holding the SS at bay were Territorial soldiers.

By 15.00 hours the Leibstandarte's 3rd Battalion had fought its way into the south-western corner of Wormhoudt and the relaxing of pressure which that advance achieved enabled SS Oberscharführer Oberschelp's patrol, belonging to 1st Battalion, to bring Dietrich and his adjutant out. The 2nd Battalion was then passed through the 3rd, and although it was involved in severe, house-to-house fighting, it had by 17.00 hours fought its way forward to the town square. The heavy and constant counter-attacks, three of them with the bayonet and one of them, allegedly, supported by tanks, were beaten off, prisoners and booty being taken. Shortly before midnight a fresh assault was launched with the intention of reaching the Oost Cappel–Rexpoude road. By dawn the Leibstandarte had reached the objective only to find that the determined enemy against whom they had been battling had been reduced to a rearguard and that the main British force had made good its escape. With the Hitler order forbidding all movement towards Dunkirk the German Army was halted around the perimeter and the Leibstandarte was posted to 3rd Panzer Division which was forming, together with three other divisions, a combat group whose task it was to launch a spoiling attack and to frustrate thereby an anticipated Allied offensive. This very successful operation was launched on 8th June. By this date it was becoming clear that the Western Allies lacked the ability to halt the German advance and, with the evacuation of the British Expeditionary Force from

Above: The Party membership book of 'Panzer' Meyer.

Below: The Stosstrupp 'Adolf Hitler', in 1923. Joseph

Berchtold leads the thirty-odd men who march under the Imperial War Flag. Note the Army pattern uniforms and the death's-head insignia on the caps.

Above: A parade in the Lichter-felde Barracks, Berlin, the Leibstandarte's home. It was once the quarters of the Imperial Cadets and was something of a military showpiece. The vast mess hall could feed 1,700 men at a time.

Below: Hitler visiting the Leibstandarte in barracks, Christmas 1935. Here he is being shown a man's locker. The office behind him is Dietrich.

Above: The band of
the Leibstandarte
playing outside the
old Chancellery on
Hitler's birthday,
1935. Under its
director of music,
Hermann Müller-
John, the band
became one of the
best in Germany
and a great
attraction at Party
functions.

Right: The
Leibstandarte
Colour-Party at the
Nuremberg Rally,
1935. The ensign
wears the distinc-
tive gorget and
bandolier.

Right: Paul Hausser, Inspector of the SS Verfügungstruppen.

Below: Dr Goebbels dining with an SS Unterscharführer of the Leibstandarte who had been wounded during the campaign in Russia, 1941. The latter's medals are the Iron Cross (Second Class), the Infantry Assault Badge in Silver and the Wounded Badge.

Left: Field Grey on Parade, 1940. Note the shoulder strap insignia.

Below: 'Sepp' Dietrich greeting Adolf Hitler at Guzow in Poland, September 1939.

Above: Men of the Leibstandarte under fire in Holland, 1940.

Left: Light refreshment during the advance through Holland, May 1940.

Opposite above: Dietrich addressing the Leibstandarte after the presentation of a new standard to the unit. Metz, August 1940.

Opposite below: An armoured car (Sd.Kfz 233) of the Reconnaissance Detachment in Greece, 1941.

Dunkirk, the French Army could only postpone but not prevent a German victory.

The Leibstandarte struck for the Aisne, driving via Soissons and Villers-Cotterêts against only token resistance from the French 11th Division. Château-Thierry fell to the 1st Battalion and, with the Weygand Line pierced, the race to the Marne began. The river was reached on 12th June and 2nd Battalion forced a crossing near St Avige. By the same evening the battalion had cut the main railway line and later that night the regiment was taken out of the line. While in billets at Etrepilly news was received that Paris had been entered and in a fever of elation the SS men rang the bells of the small, village church.

For the Germans the campaign had taken on the character of a battle of pursuit. But one check to the Leibstandarte's headlong drive south-westwards, as part of 9th Panzer Division, came on 19th June, at the Allier river, a tributary of the Oise, but the SS forced a bridgehead near Moulins and pushed fast reconnaissance detachments ahead of the main body to seize the bridge across the Sioule at St Pourcain. At the bridge French troops were seen furiously trying to build a barricade. There were too few SS infantry available and the element of surprise had to be the chief weapon. The commander of a motor-cycle point detachment ordered SS Obersturmführer Knittel to rush the defences. In a short, sharp, cycle assault, covered by fire from a pair of reconnaissance vehicles and mortar teams, the barricade was forced but the bridge was blown in the faces of the attackers. The battalion's main effort was then switched south of Pourcain, and within a short time Jochen Peiper, of 3rd Battalion's point company, reported that a crossing had been forced. The defenders of Pourcain were rolled up and the capture of Gannat at 16.00 hours preceded a drive on Vichy. During the advance on the French spa town an artillery column was overrun and captured, and demolitions so obstructed the move forward that it was not until dusk that Vichy was reached and contact established with the German troops who had captured it.

The chase was carried forward on 20th June by 2nd Battalion, which captured the aerodrome at Clermont-Ferrand together with a vast haul of planes, including fighter aircraft from a Polish squadron, as well as eight tanks and thousands of prisoners. The Leibstandarte was then pulled out of the line for a two-day rest and was then put in again to press the assault towards St Etienne. Just outside the town the SS encountered a strong defence centred around a group of First World War tanks. The armour on these veterans was resistant to the 37mm anti-tank gun and heavier artillery had to be called for. The French tanks were finally driven off but the town was not entered until 24th June when it fell to 1st Battalion. The signing of the Armistice ended the campaign in the West and the Leibstandarte was moved out of what became Vichy France into the German-held sector. A proposed victory march in Paris did not take place and the Regiment was then moved to Metz where it lay in garrison from July 1941 to February 1942. The term 'lay in garrison' does not imply a life of idleness; on the contrary the period was one of refitting and retraining. An armoured reconnaissance battalion was raised and added to the establishment and integrated exercises by all arms were intensively practised.

The Balkan Campaign

On 28th October 1940, in a move which surprised the German leader, the armies of Fascist Italy invaded Greece. The military reverses which the Italians then suffered compelled them to ask Germany for military aid which was soon forthcoming. The German High Command had prepared a plan, the execution of which would deny Greece to the British as an advanced base and would also assist Mussolini by destroying the Greek Army. Two German armies, Second and Twelfth, were moved into position and it was with this latter Army that the Leibstandarte served during the Balkan campaign.

At the beginning of February 1941 the SS unit was moved from Alsace via Campalung in Romania and thence to Bulgaria from which country the Twelfth Army was to strike towards Skoplje in southern Jugoslavia. That country too was to be invaded and occupied by the Germans. The most difficult feature of military operations in the mountainous areas of the Balkans was that of the shortage of roads and railways. The German planners solved this logistical problem by loading rafts with supplies and towing them down the Danube. In this way huge amounts of ammunition, equipment and supplies were built up for the divisions of Twelfth Army.

Hostilities opened in the light of a new moon and on 6th April the Leibstandarte, forming part of XXXX Corps, followed 9th Panzer Division in its drive from the border town of Kustendil. The Corps assault was made by two columns. In the northern arm was 9th Panzer supported by the Leibstandarte. The task of this group was to force the Kriva Pass and to capture Skoplje some sixty miles inside Jugoslavia. This had been accomplished by the evening of the 7th and the column spent the following day consolidating the gains which it had made. The southern arm, meanwhile, made up of 73rd Infantry Division, had captured the strategically important town of Prilep and had sent out patrols to link up with the Italian forces to the west of the country.

The speed, suddenness and force of the German drive

had shattered Jugoslav resistance and the Vardar river
line was taken on the afternoon of the first day. The
Jugoslav Army had been neither strong nor modern
enough to withstand the German onslaught, nor had its
divisions been correctly disposed. By the morning of 9th
April a link-up had been made with the Italians and the
Leibstandarte, now spearheading the Corps advance,
swung south to support 73rd Division. Orders were
received for the next move by XXXX Corps. This was to
force the Monastir Gap, the 3,000ft-high Javat Pass
twenty miles to the west of Monastir and to effect another
link with the Italian Army. This area was the gateway to
Greece and in order to produce the maximum shock
effect Witt's 1st Battalion was reinforced. In addition to
the motorized infantry there were now two troops of anti-
tank guns (one each of 37mm and 50mm), one troop of
light field howitzers, two troops of infantry guns (one light
and one heavy), a battery of 88mm guns and a company
of engineers.

The reinforced drive broke through the positions of the
mixed Australian Brigade Group and into the entrance to
the Klidi Pass. The SS soldiers spent the night in bitter
cold and snow waiting for dawn and for the artillery
barrage which would smash the British positions on the
mountain crests. Under cover of the barrage the engineers
began to clear the minefields and to let the tanks of 9th
Panzer Division advance while the Leibstandarte men
fought hand-to-hand battles to drive the British and
Imperial troops from their positions. All day long the
noise of battle rolled round the mountains of northern
Greece but by mid-day of the 12th the pass had been
forced and eighty prisoners, the first of the 600 men who
were to be taken in this battle, were captured. These were
men of 2/4th Australian Battalion and for most of the
Leibstandarte these were the first Imperial troops they

had ever seen '. . . some of the prisoners coming down were mercenaries [Söldner] from Australia. They do not behave like the cold English, except in their arrogance and this is more external. They do not seem to be as well disciplined as the English nor do they wear their uniform as a soldier should. They were complaining of the cold for they have just arrived here from Egypt.'

On the 13th the troops of Witt's battle group had swung through the hills, outflanked the defence and emerged from the south-eastern exit of the pass. A British armoured counter-attack drove in the forward Leibstandarte company but a pair of 88mm guns, hastily towed into position, soon restored the situation.

For the loss of only thirty-seven killed, ninety-eight wounded and two missing the SS had captured the key to the Allied position in northern Greece and ahead lay a pursuit across the plain towards the Klissura Pass. The Leibstandarte turned towards Lake Kastoria and the pass which was held by part of 21st Greek Infantry Division. Extensive demolitions slowed the pace and bitter, minor clashes occurred along the entire length of the narrow road, the only passage through the hills. The SS troops of the point section halted under a concentrated barrage of shells and bullets as they ascended the mountain slopes. No armour could be brought up yet and even the artillery could find no level ground from which to fire their pieces to support the attack. This would be a battle in which the SS riflemen would be fighting like mountain troops. Small combat groups from the Leibstandarte's reconnaissance battalion under SS Sturmbannführer Kurt Meyer formed up and made their way to the summit. Those who went along goat trails carried only their personal weapons but others, managing to advance across less difficult country, carried mortars and other support weapons. Silently the parties of SS men worked round the Allied flank but the moon was down and the groups began to straggle and to lose cohesion. The assault was then delayed until all the parties had concentrated and in the cold light of an April dawn, covered by the fire of a battery of 88mm guns whose crews risked going over the edge of a precipice with every round which was fired, the Leibstandarte infantry went in with a rush. The Greek defenders fought with savage determination but under the pressure of the German assault resistance began to crumble and soon hundreds of prisoners, including a brigadier and three battalion commanders, had been taken. By 15th April the road was open. The patrols sent out towards Lake Kastoria met a determined Greek rearguard from 12th Infantry Division and the Greek Cavalry Division; the German advance halted. In pouring rain the Leibstandarte's 3rd Battalion captured the important Height 800 and, covered by a Stuka dive-bombing attack, had captured the town by late afternoon. 12,000 prisoners were taken in the first days.

The advance of the Leibstandarte was then directed to the south-east flank so as to attempt an outflanking movement along the Servia but rain and demolitions slowed the advance to such an extent that the move was overtaken and new orders were issued. These directed that on 19th April the Division was to advance south-westwards from Gravena to Joannina so as to cut off the Greek units manning the line. The Mesovan Pass was captured, this move not only covering the open flank of Twelfth Army but at the same time isolating the Greek units on the west side of the Pindus mountains. The knowledge that the Leibstandarte was blocking the line of withdrawal of the Greek Army compelled the Greek leaders to sue for an armistice and on 21st April the armies of the Centre, of Western Macedonia and of the Epirus surrendered.

The only organized resistance was now that being offered by the British and Imperial forces and the pursuit of those troops began on 24th April. The Leibstandarte moved out from Arta and in a relentless drive of over 180 miles, across the Pindus mountains, the SS troops arrived at the Straits of Corinth to find that the British had eluded them by evacuation. Determined to pursue their enemy Meyer, the Leibstandarte Reconnaissance Battalion commander, commandeered a pair of fishing boats and ran a ferry service from Navpaktos bringing the whole of the advanced guard across the water. On the 27th the Division moved down the west coast of the Peloponnese and reached Pirgos, where part of 3rd Battalion captured men of 3rd Royal Tank Regiment, before advancing farther south in the peninsula. A unit of the Reconnaissance Battalion cleared the southern coast of the Gulf of Corinth and established a link-up with paratroopers from 2nd Fallschirmjäger Regiment who had been fighting at the Corinth Canal. This link-up ended the three-week long Balkan campaign, so far as the Leibstandarte was concerned, and following a victory parade in Athens the SS troops returned to barracks in Czechoslovakia to refit and to prepare for the next campaigns which it was certain would be fought in the summer of 1941.

5

Military Operations – 'Barbarossa': The Invasion of Russia

Directive No. 21

On 22nd June 1941, the German radio broadcast to the world the news that the German Armed Forces had crossed the Russo-German frontier. Almost four years elapsed before the Russian High Command was able to report that the last, armed, German soldier had been expelled from Soviet soil. The history of the war in the East between those times is more than just a record of a clash of armies; far more than a conflict of ideologies. The Germans, and specifically the SS, saw it as a battle of civilization; the European versus the 'Asian' and, in that sense, a repetition of the struggle between the East and West which has shaped European history since Byzantium. It was seen as a latter-day Crusade and the SS went into the campaign with high hearts. Ideologically, National Socialism was contesting with Communism; economically, Germany needed the Eastern oil and grain, and the Leibstandarte would capture them for the Führer. Militarily, the time had come to neutralize the menace on the Eastern flank, for as early as July 1940 Hitler had declared his intention to wage war against Russia. His Directive No. 21 set in motion the active planning and preparations for that war under the code-name of 'Barbarossa'.

For the campaign there were to be three Army Groups, North, Centre and South, and it was with the latter that the Leibstandarte spent the years of its three tours of duty. We who live west of the Rhine had limited military horizons during the Second World War. Battle lines were shorter and numbers involved relatively few in comparison to the vast distances and masses of people involved in the East. There the front, at one time, ran for over 2,000 miles, from the woods and snows of northern Finland, through the wide steppe land of Central Russia to the high mountains and sub-tropical climate of the Caucasus. The opening campaign for war on such a scale required on the German side the movement and maintenance of millions of men, 600,000 vehicles, 750,000 horses, more than 7,000 pieces of artillery and 3,000 tanks. During February 1941 the first divisions which were to form Army Group South began to concentrate along the frontier. In March the total was sixteen, by May thirty-nine had been gathered and by June the forty-six divisions which made up Army Group South closed up to the border. Army Group South, composed of Sixth, Eleventh and Seventeenth Armies, and supported by 1st Panzer Group, had the task of cutting off and destroying the Red Armies west of the Dnieper. The vital role of the Panzer Group, situated on the left flank, was to break through below Kovel. Then by fast movement it was to throw pincer arms around the Russian armies of the South-West Front and hold them fast in an armoured grip until they had been destroyed.

With hindsight it is clear to see that Army Group South had insufficient strength to carry out its allotted tasks. It held a line from the southern edge of the Pripet Marshes to the Black Sea and the first bound it had to make was from the frontier to the Dnieper, an advance of no less than 300 miles, and to Rostov, the main objective, it was 700 miles. All these advances were to be made across a region poor in communications and on roads so bad that two hours' rain would turn them into swamps sufficient to bog down a tank column. And there was, of course, also the Red Army.

The German Army's new opponent was to a very large degree an unknown factor and intelligence appreciations, both of the fighting ability of the Red Army as well as of the vast Russian resources in material and manpower, were wildly underestimated. The belief that the forthcoming campaign would be a short one was reinforced by the poor showing of the Red Army *vis-à-vis* the Finns in the winter of 1939–40.

A German High Command Memorandum, issued shortly before the opening of hostilities, listed as the main defects of the Red Army at Command level that there was 'slowness, lack of decision and inadequate organization', but the report paid tribute to the 'endurance, tenacity and [to] offensive spirit of the Red Army as a whole'. Paradoxically it was this offensive spirit which was a built-in defect, for the Russian commanders had had no training in carrying out a fighting retreat and in the first months of the war mismanaged their encircled armies. There was scant consideration for the individual in the Red Army; the infantry was sacrificed in hopeless attacks and officers who failed to achieve given objectives often paid for their failure with their life.

Despite these shortcomings the Red Army was a powerful force which, even with only partial mobilization, mustered more than 130 rifle divisions. The tank strength of the opposing armies gave the Russians with 10,000 vehicles a three-to-one numerical superiority, and with the appearance of the T34 a technical one, for this was a tank against which the German front-line troops, initially, were impotent. In June 1941 the Red Army was horse orientated, as were most European armies of that period, and according to Intelligence there were less than a million motor vehicles in the whole of Russia. Thus, in the first battles the pace of the horse and of the foot soldier generally dictated the speed of Russian movement.

The Soviet High Command's defensive plan saw the southern as the decisive front and placed the greatest concentration of its forces there. Originally under the command of General Kirponos and then, from 10th July, under Marshal Budyenni, the South-Western Front disposed, according to German Intelligence sources, sixty-nine rifle, eleven cavalry and twenty-eight armoured divisions. This massive force was defending a rich agricultural area, not extensively wooded; a flat land suitable for fast, tank movement. The river lines of the Pruth, San and Bug and Dnieper formed the main, natural obstacles to an invader, with the Dnieper as the strongest defence line, for at Kiev it was three-quarters of a mile wide. Along the old 1939 frontier ran the man-made defensive system of the 'Stalin Line'.

Supporting the Red Army in the field were the guerrilla fighters in the German rear. The Russian use of partisan forces confirmed Kurt Meyer's statement, 'Now the front is everywhere', for their activities drained combat strength from the main front lines to fight them and tied down whole divisions of troops. In those regions where the local population had established a *modus vivendi* with the occupying forces, partisan units carried out acts of sabotage and atrocity against the Germans in the hope of provoking retaliation against the passive local population and thereby recruiting new partisans.

This action/reaction helped to produce the harshness, the brutality and the contempt for human life which characterized the war on the Eastern Front. Who was responsible for the first atrocity, the first unnecessary brutal action cannot now, and probably never could be, established positively. But it is certain that between the SS as a whole and Soviets there was engendered a special hatred which forced both sides to take up attitudes which permitted of no compromise and it was also certain that this Soviet hatred was particularly strong against those units whose men wore the cuff-band with the name of the German leader.

Within days of the start of the campaign the men of the Leibstandarte were convinced that their wounded who had fallen into Soviet hands had been the victims of summary and brutal execution. To prevent the badly wounded from the possibility of being tortured it then became an accepted practice for officers to give the *coup de grâce* to those of their men who could not be removed from the battlefield – and it was a matter of honour to evacuate those who could be moved. On the Eastern Front life was not held to be so dear and the SS shot, often summarily, Communists, commissars, partisans and other disruptive elements. It soon became widely accepted that the SS could pacify a district of partisan activity more quickly and more effectively than the Army security units.

The new D-Day dawned and on 21st June an Order of the Day was issued to the German Army stressing the danger of the Red Menace to Western civilization. The new Crusade had begun. Three million Germans, superior in technology but inferior in numbers and potential, were facing four and a half million Russians who were to a large extent unprepared and not as proficient as their opponents. The mass of the Red Army had had almost no military experience; the bulk of the German Army had fought four successful campaigns since 1939.

The position of the Leibstandarte as part of III Corps had been determined in May but, as a result of a shortage of spares for its tracked vehicles, it was unable to complete its concentration and was posted to XIV Corps of 1st Panzer Group, in the Lublin area. On 21st June the SS unit began to unload and to prepare itself for action.

The Warning Order from Panzer Group fixing H-Hour and D-Day had no relevance to the Leibstandarte, which remained uncommitted until 27th June, and on that day it swung out of the concentration area, down the road to Ostrowiec following closely behind the SS 'Viking' Division. A short period as strategic reserve to Panzer Group then followed and, at last, the Leibstandarte moved from the area of Sandomierz to a sector south-west of Zamość where, early in the morning of 1st July, the main body crossed the Vistula and reached the former frontier line.

The Leibstandarte was about to begin the first of three tours of combat duty in Russia and this first mission was to keep it on active service until June 1942.

'We have swept the Tommies from the Continent,' wrote one keen SS man during the period of waiting around Lublin. 'But it seems as if this campaign will be fought without us. Our section hopes that we are being held back for some really special task – something worthy of us', and it was with such sentiments that the men and vehicles of the Leibstandarte rolled forward into the wide steppe lands of Galicia and the west Ukraine.

The First Russian Campaign: July 1941 to June 1942

By the time that the Leibstandarte entered in upon Operation 'Barbarossa' the opening battles were showing success and the two arms of 1st Panzer Group pincer, sweeping aside Russian armoured resistance, were driving forward; the one upon Kiev and the second towards Kasatin.

The vehicles of the Leibstandarte rolled forward in the pride of a fine summer morning towards Luck, and soon the whole regiment was deeply involved in frontier battles in west Ukraine, combating Soviet tank units trying to cut the Northern Highway at Dubno and Olyka. As the

Russian armoured wedges stormed from Moszkov SS gunners took them in flank and drove them back in confusion. Heavy rain in the evening soaked the battle-field but failed to dampen the spirits of the young SS soldiers at the end of the first day's hostilities. A diary entry records Soviet tactics: 'Their counter-attack . . . was launched while we were still getting our breath back. Their infantry came in mounted on open lorries which swayed from side to side with the speed. It looked as if all the Ivans on the trucks were standing up and firing their guns at us. The whole thing was quite primitive. The lorries just drove straight at our positions . . . a shell hit a lorry and killed many of the infantry mounted on it, but the others sprang over the side and charged us on foot . . . There was no cover at all . . . They had no hope of reaching our positions, but they still came on . . .'

The Soviet attacks to cut the Corps supply line, the Northern Highway, continued for several days and the Leibstandarte, having captured Moszkov, was then ordered to form front on the Rovno–Luck line to hold the Russian thrusts from the Borbin sector. Heavy rain had turned the roads into rivers of mud and the Leibstandarte could not complete the move as a cohesive force. In addition to the bad weather and the enemy opposition Seventeenth Army was now involved in fighting through the defences of the Stalin Line, to achieve space to manoeuvre so that 1st Panzer Group might be unleashed again. With this object achieved the armour raced ahead, without pause or let-up, across the Russian steppe land, outstripping, in some cases by as much as fifty miles, the supporting infantry, thrusting into the unknown. The intoxication of those days is recalled by the letter of one armoured car commander, who, having described the emptiness of the steppe, continues: 'Our situation map shows that we are fighting in a sort of vacuum. We cannot stop and wait for them [the infantry] to catch up. We must push ahead . . . we are a storm wind.' The wide dispersion of the German thrusts left open flanks into which the Soviets attacked trying to cut off the armoured spearhead from the infantry. To plug one such gap on the northern flank of 11th Panzer Division, the Leibstandarte moved upon Ostrog and at midday on 7th July the point units, leading the Advanced Guard, crossed the river Sluczk, burst out of the confines of the bridgehead, smashed through the defences of the Stalin Line at Miropol and thrust up the road towards Zhitomir. At Romanovka in the densely wooded region north of the Highway, the spearhead detachments met severe opposition and had to fight alone and unsupported against an enemy numerically superior in men and tanks. Back at the Sluczk river the main body of the unit was struggling forward under constant air assault, but by evening it had closed up on the point units east of Romanovka.

Supreme Headquarters viewed the course of the operations with optimism and Halder, Chief of the General Staff, considered that Army Group South had achieved its given task of destroying the mass of the enemy forces west of the Dnieper. The front-line soldiers were not so sanguine. The fighting had been hard and bitter against the Red infantry but a new factor had then been introduced against which they were impotent. Russian tank replacements to cover the losses suffered in the first weeks of fighting had begun to reach the battlefield and these replacements included the T34 whose hardened armour and sloping angles made it immune to any of the weapons in the infantry arsenal. Even the 88mm field gun could only penetrate the T34 at ranges below a thousand yards and the morale of the German troops, even of the élite Leibstandarte, suffered from the knowledge that they were powerless against this Russian weapon.

Soviet assaults came in against the thin SS line and the situation continued critical until the infantry, marching incredible distances each day, arrived to thicken the battle front and to relieve the pressure upon 1st Panzer Group, which was then withdrawn into reserve and regrouped. The Leibstandarte, however, remained in the fight and was involved, on 8th July, in an operation to capture the important Kudnov road junction. The action, fought to clear more of the Northern Highway, was carried out by the Reconnaissance Battalion advancing under a barrage laid by the 88mm artillery batteries. Less than an hour after the leading elements had stormed towards the Russian positions the river Teterev had been crossed, the junction, about twelve miles west of Zhitomir, had been taken, and the beaten enemy given no respite as the exultant SS pursued him through Marshilevsk, up to and across the Highway.

Unknown to the men of the Leibstandarte the Russian armies on the whole South-Western Front were going over to a counter-offensive and the centre of this massive stroke was directed upon the Northern Highway, the Corps supply line. It was as urgent for the Russians to cut this as it was essential for the Germans to keep it open. Soviet attacks came in almost hourly; the first, at 11.00 hours, reached the Highway but then collapsed in the storm of fire poured upon the attackers by the SS men. 'These must have been élite troops . . . nearly as good as us', and the writer goes on to describe the Red Army's determination to win, expressed in bayonet charges and in savage hand-to-hand fighting. 'We did training in close combat back in the golden days, but we always thought it somewhat superfluous. We don't now . . . they use their entrenching tools like the Storm Troops of the Great War. These are the best fighters we have ever met . . . better even than the Poles. How long ago all that seems.'

The attack at 01.00 hours was literally man-to-man with the SS and the Soviets stabbing and hacking at each other in the dark forests. Around them and in the tops of the trees mortar bombs burst showering German and Russian alike with lethal shrapnel. The losses suffered during this two-day battle exceeded, according to Meyer, the total casualties of all the other campaigns.

The situation at all levels was confused and confusing. Every German thrust encountered a Russian counter-thrust, every blow met a riposte, every pincer found itself outflanked by a Soviet arm. In desperation one Panzer commander asked: '. . . are the Russians outflanking us or are we outflanking them?'.

Temporarily Soviet pressure eased and the SS, quick to exploit an advantage, cleared Shepkova during a night attack on 9th July and took the assault past the town in a north-westerly direction towards Zhitomir. Contact with Panzer Group headquarters was lost but Fieseler Storch Co-operation aircraft located the forward elements and Luftwaffe pilots could report that they had reached Zhitomir and that the Soviets were in full flight. The strategic plan had reached the stage at which Army Group was capable of seizing Kiev, the Ukrainian capital, but Hitler changed his mind and, on 10th July, directed the main effort to be made on Uman. The bulk of Sixth Army then struck south-east to cut off the Soviets fighting against Eleventh and Seventeenth Armies and the Leibstandarte, holding the northern flank, came under assault from several of the nine divisions of Fifth Red Army which were making a blow against Sixth Army's left flank. Under this overwhelming pressure the northern wing of Army Group went, temporarily, over to the defensive, but by the 21st the offensive was resumed again and the advance continued towards Uman. During the week of fierce fighting which marked the resumption of the offensive and the repulse of the Red divisions attacking from Korosten and the Pripet Marshes, the Leibstandarte's aggressive action rescued the 16th Panzer Division from serious difficulty. No less than three Soviet tank divisions attacked the 16th Panzer and only the intervention of the SS, moving on to the exposed left flank of the Panzer Division, and striking across the Sokolovka road, helped to overcome the crisis. Pushing down from the Sokolovka road towards Panji List the Leibstandarte drove southwards, down the Konela river, west of the Sokolovka–Uman road, and then, on 29th July, switched across country to continue the thrust down the eastern side of the road.

That the Russians could bring up no less than three armoured divisions against one single German division was an indication that Soviet resources were greater than Intelligence had estimated. The optimistic Halder calculated on 23rd July that Russian losses had reached 50 per cent and that German losses had been 20 per cent in infantry and 50 per cent in armour. The true facts, that many Panzer divisions had been reduced to only 20 per cent of their establishments, seem to have been unknown to the Chief of the German General Staff. Nor does he seem to have appreciated that the supply of reinforcements to the Russian armies had brought them back to a strength as great as, if not greater than, that with which they had begun the campaign. In Halder's view the Red Army was weakening. Had he known that two Ukrainian divisions had refused to go up the line, then this knowledge would have confirmed his faulty appreciation. His belief was that the whole Russian South-Western Front was cracking, but once again what seemed evident to the Staff at Headquarters was not borne out by the experience of the SS soldiers in their slit trenches, for the advance upon Uman was encountering increased resistance. Continuous fighting brought the Leibstandarte through the Zibermanovka district to Lechnovka but the Soviet garrison fought hard and with determination to break through the ring which Panzer Group had thrown round them and brought the SS drive to a halt.

By the end of July the advanced Panzer spearheads were drawing near to Uman and the fall of Nova Archangelsk hastened the closing of a ring around the Red Sixth and Twelfth Armies. The fighting continued bitter and the Soviet defenders fought to the last round; many units fought to the last man, too. Counter-attacks to break the German encirclement were heavy and continuous: '. . . we are all exhausted from lack of sleep. We seem to have been fighting without adequate sleep for weeks now . . . I've lost all track of time . . . Yesterday their cavalry charged our recce vehicles just after we had driven off break-through attempts by their armoured cars . . .' Stronger attacks using tanks came in against the Leibstandarte battalions and succeeded, for a short time, in smashing a gap in the SS lines and re-entering the town. At dawn a mass infantry assault was launched against the exhausted SS soldiers but this attack was smashed before it had really begun in the fire of 21cm mortars which had been brought up.

Flinging one armoured pincer south-east from Kasalin the 1st Panzer Group linked up with armoured elements of a Magyar infantry division and closed the ring fast around the twenty-five Red divisions. With the reduction of this vast pocket more than 100,000 Russian soldiers poured into captivity. The part played by the Leibstandarte in this vast and hard-fought battle had been of great significance and already Hitler's Guard was being asked for when difficult military tasks had to be resolved.

Kempf, the General commanding the corps of which

the Leibstandarte was then a part, wrote: 'Since 24/7, the Leibstandarte SS Adolf Hitler has taken the most glorious part in the encirclement of the enemy around Uman. Committed at the focus of the battle for the seizure of the key enemy position at Archangelsk, the Leibstandarte . . . with incomparable dash, took the city and the heights to the south. In the spirit of the most devoted brotherhood of arms, they intervened on their own initiative in the arduous struggle of the 16th Infantry Division (motorized) on their left flank and routed the enemy, destroying numerous tanks.

'Today at the conclusion of the battle of annihilation around Uman, I want to recognize and express my special thanks to the Leibstandarte SS Adolf Hitler for their exemplary effort and incomparable bravery.

'The battles around Archangelsk will be recorded indelibly and forever in the war history of the Leibstandarte . . .'

Such was the unsolicited testimony of an army general.

With the fall of Uman the Panzer Group stormed towards new objectives. Bobry, heavily defended by 12th Cavalry Division, fell to the SS on 9th August and the advance was driven towards Nikolaev. The crossroads town of Sasselje, set in a very attractive area of small lakes, was captured from its defenders who included an infantry and a cavalry division. At Sasselje the Leibstandarte position formed a salient and Russian troops moved upon the town from the west, thinking of it as an escape route and unaware that it was in German hands. The Red columns were smashed by artillery fire as they moved up the road, were halted and driven back leaving a trail of blazing trucks to mark their retreat. The Soviet commanders to the east and west of the Leibstandarte spearhead brought in co-ordinated assaults; sometimes simultaneously, sometimes alternately. An infantry assault from the east burst out of the maize and sunflower fields and poured like a human wave towards the SS lines, only to be driven back with heavy loss. From the west came a tank assault, supported by infantry. The Leibstandarte field artillery destroyed the armoured thrust and the German reconnaissance vehicles drove into the Red infantry mass, throwing it back in confusion. Driving the broken Russian units before them the SS pushed southwards from Sasselje during the morning of 17th August, reached Snigirevka during the early evening and, bypassing this strongly garrisoned town, roared on towards Cherson, a large industrial city and the final objective of this particular offensive. Street fighting, house to house battles; in some desperate engagements combat in single rooms; these were the order of the day as Soviet Marines fought man-to-man with Leibstandarte soldiers for possession of the town. During the late afternoon of the 20th the SS were able to hand over their sector and moved into reserve.

On 21st August the Seventeenth Army crossed the Dnieper and established a firm bridgehead, but it was not until the first week of September that the Leibstandarte crossed the three-quarter mile wide river with orders to advance across the Nogai steppe. The vast depressing emptiness of that region is reflected in the diary which records: 'There is very little water and what there is is salty. Coffee is salt flavoured, the soup is oversalted . . . but we are pleased even to get this tepid liquid for this is true desert country. Movement is visible for miles; clouds of choking, red brown dust hang over our moving columns and pinpoint our exact positions. Paradoxically the only signs of life are the dead tree trunks of telegraph poles. Without them it would be difficult to orientate oneself . . . sometimes we find a melon field and gorge, but the unripe ones have unhappy effects . . .'

The drive continued from Novya Mayatschka, which had fallen on 9th September, to a combined Army and SS pincer movement, across the steppe to Kalantchak. Orders to carry out a night attack to capture the town were countermanded. Instead, an immediate move on the Crimea was ordered. Two days later the columns of Leibstandarte vehicles had pushed south of Novo Alexandrovka and were moving via Admaniy upon the village of Preobrachenko.

During this time another ring was thrown around the Russians and when, on 14th September, the 3rd, 9th and 16th Panzer Divisions met at Lochivna, sixty Soviet divisions belonging to five Red armies were cut off. But the Soviet High Command was still bringing up fresh troops to areas outside the area of encirclement and the Leibstandarte met increasing resistance as it moved on the line Militopol–Nikopol towards the Crimea. The Russian armies which had withdrawn into the peninsula could have been contained for destruction at some later date but Hitler decided otherwise and dissipated the effort of Army Group South as well as extending the length of the front by his insistence that the Crimea be captured.

One of the entrances to the peninsula was the thin neck of land, only five miles wide, known as the Perekop narrows. This vital position was devoid of cover, heavily fortified and strongly manned. The new task of the Leibstandarte was to force the passage. The first attack rolled via Preobrachenko but then the offensive came to a halt in the face of a defence lying secure behind minefields and supported by an armoured train. The Perekop narrows could not be forced. With their efforts blocked at the western opening the SS swung the main point of their attack to the eastern passage at Balykov. Under cover of a thick dawn fog the assault detachments drove into the attack and by 09.00 hours had broken through the defence lines and captured Sliakov station and the town of Novo Alesksovka. With the assault pushed to Genichek the Leibstandarte stood on the shores of the Sea of Azov. The town of Genichek, located on a plateau, dominated the surrounding countryside and the Russian counter-attack preparations were made under Leibstandarte observation. When the attacks came in, every man being visible to the SS observers, a hail of fire was brought down upon the luckless Soviet soldiers, smashing their attacks before they came within striking distance of the German lines. With the Russian attacks broken the time had come for the advance to be continued along the northern shore of the sea towards Melitopol. The leading elements of the Leibstandarte reached Rodionovka on 18th September and took up defensive positions with the right flank anchored on Lake Moloch-noye. The thinly held line was subjected to assaults by waves of Red troops who poured from the Soviet bridge-head on the western bank of the Molochnoye river. Many of the SS soldiers considered that the fighting on that day had been the hardest that they had had to meet.

The advance upon Melitopol required four whole days, for not the least of the Leibstandarte's difficulties was caused by the loose, sandy soil which bogged down the wheeled vehicles and clogged the motor engines. But then came recall orders and on 21st September a twelve-hour drive brought the main body of the Leibstandarte back, once again, to the western entrance to the Crimea. The task of LIV Corps and especially of the SS Leibstandarte was to attempt again to force the Perekop narrows, but on 27th September the Ninth and Eighteenth Red Armies flung themselves into a counter-attack, destroying the Romanian troops who were facing them and driving deep into the rear areas. The full weight of the offensive was in

the north and to meet it the Leibstandarte was switched
from Nish Serogosy, in the extreme southern sector, to
Gavrilovka, on the outer left flank, to be the linchpin of
the defence. The first counter to the Red advance was to
put a company across the Dnieper and to form a bridgehead at Kamenka. This small outpost would break up the
first enemy assaults and be a base for future offensive
operations. The second counter to the Red offensive was
to contain the Russian tank columns which were rampag-
ing twenty-five miles behind the main battle line. A
Russian magazine editorial exhorted the soldiers of the
Red Army to drive the German bandits out of the
Ukraine and to stop them from entering the beautiful
Crimea. The Dnieper was supposed to have flowed red
with blood and to have been bridged with German
corpses.

Despite these exhortations the Red armies crumbled
under the thrust mounted by the SS and the German
Alpine troops. The counter-offensive went in on 30th
September, and from the town of Dnieperovka, on the
Leibstandarte's left flank, the advance struck eastwards,
across an anti-tank ditch at Elisabetovka and on to Balki.

The vigorous thrust by the crack German units smashed
into the flank of the over-extended Soviet assault and the
Soviets had insufficient power to defend themselves
against the German counter-thrust. The Dnieper bridgehead burst open and von Kleist's 1st Panzer Group, now
renamed First Panzer Army, thrust towards Rostov with
the intent of catching and destroying the enemy in a wide,
encircling movement. The essence of this pursuit battle,
carried out across appalling terrain scored by numerous
rivers, is contained in a phrase in another diary entry:
'. . . we can move faster across the open steppe than they
can . . .' At certain points the Red Army rearguards
stood at bay, attempting to delay the German drive. The
sacrifice of Red infantry was on an unbelievable scale,

particularly at Jellisavetovka, where, in the early days of October, the Leibstandarte point detachments ran into a series of bitter counter-attacks. These were a foretaste of the fighting to come in the area between Melitopol and the Dnieper. The defence by the Soviet rearguards had given the defenders of Melitopol time to construct an elaborate and deep defence system, the backbone of which was a wide anti-tank ditch set behind extensive minefields, but by 5th October the *élan* of the SS drive had proved to be irresistible and the whole Russian front broke open. 'We were in among them like Hussars cutting down broken infantry . . . nothing could stop our advance. We passed whole batteries of guns, columns of marching troops moving east. No time to disarm them; a quick "Ryki vertch" (hands up), a gesture towards the west and on we roared again. Numbers? – who knows how many we took.'

At Terpinye masses of Russian soldiers and vehicles were struggling to cross the Dnieper by a single bridge. The appearance on the western bank of the Leibstandarte's 1st and Reconnaissance Battalions was the signal for the Soviets to blow the bridge, crowded though it was with their own men. The SS point units drove a passage across a mined ford to carry the advance forward without delay.

Taganrog, the target of First Panzer Army, lay on a far distant horizon, but Stalino, the objective of the Leibstandarte and of an Alpine unit, was by Eastern Front distances only a stone's throw away – barely 250 miles from the start-line. Intelligence reported that the defence of the SS objective had been entrusted to fresh, Siberian troops. The Soviets were obviously preparing for the coming winter fighting.

The pursuit battles were fought at Romanovka, where the Reconnaissance Battalion missed the opportunity of

capturing a Red Army commander, and at the port of
Berdyansk. The next, immediate objective was Mariupol,
the capture of which would pin the Soviets against the Sea
of Azov. The excitements and crises of those days are
recorded in the diary only in note form but mention is
made of fighting in the dried-up bed of a river. The
German fire and the high river banks caused the Red
Army terrible losses and resistance broke so completely
that panic broke out among the trapped Russian units.
'Panzer' Meyer's account of using petrol to destroy a
Russian T34 is paralleled by the same writer describing
the tactics which were beginning to be worked out by SS
units enabling a man with an explosive charge to destroy
a tank in single combat. These tactics were developed to
such a degree that 'tank stalking' became almost a sport.

The Leibstandarte assault passed across the rolling,
treeless countryside, through Berdyansk, through a line
of fortifications outside Mariupol and towards the city.
Along the arrow-straight roads the SS vehicles hurtled,
beating off opposition, and burst into Mariupol. There
was street fighting of varying lengths of time and of
various degrees of bitterness, but the town passed into the
hands of the SS attackers. The Battle of the Sea of Azov
was over.

On 11th October began the battle for Taganrog and
five days after the offensive opened 1st Battalion had
established a bridgehead across the Mius river at
Koselkin, through which the rest of the unit passed,
striking towards Taganrog. The 2nd Battalion, holding its
position in the bridgehead on the 1st Battalion's left flank,
came under severe pressure from a Red tank regiment
and suffered heavy loss before the attackers were driven
off and the situation restored.

Taganrog fell on the 17th and three days later the
Leibstandarte was able to report the capture of Stalino.

Throughout the following weeks heavy and incessant rain first slowed and then halted the German advance and although a move was made against Rostov immediately after the occupation of Stalino it was not until the middle of November that III Corps had reached the area of that town. During these weeks of rain, mud and misery the Leibstandarte lying in defensive positions west of Rostov was made aware of the difficulties which lay ahead. Severe dysentery, bronchitis and other lung infections swept through the regiment and losses by sickness reduced rifle companies to a level where the men were almost continually on sentry duty, usually exposed to inclement weather and without regular food supplies.

The critical situation in which the German Army found itself placed the chief strain upon the front-line soldier. The logistical difficulties, the difference in gauge between Russian and German railway tracks, the absence of roads, the destruction of bridges and the ever increasing interference from guerrilla fighters all combined to cut off the combat units from their bases. The infantry, many of whom had marched 1,000 miles in the first four weeks of the campaign, were without boots or socks. Casualties and sickness were wasting the Army faster than replacements could reach the front-line and companies numbered fewer than fifty men, a quarter of their war establishment. One thousand horses a day were being lost on the Eastern Front, no vehicle spares were coming up and the Red Army, which seemed to thrive in adverse conditions, was counter-attacking the open, northern flank of 1st Panzer Army. And real winter was yet to come, although frosts had begun in the first November days and the opening day of the final assault on Rostov had seen the first prolonged and heavy snowfall.

On 17th November, III Panzer Corps, with the Leibstandarte under command, opened the assault on Rostov.

The conditions under which this battle was fought made it an even more difficult one than usual. Snow covered the minefields; the intense, biting cold destroyed concentration and units lost direction in the blizzard which blew. Russian armoured attacks, prepared defences, fresh and well-equipped Soviet troops – all were met, struck and destroyed. By 20th November, Rostov had fallen to III Corps and an important contribution to the success of the battle was the capture of the Don railway bridge by men of the SS Reconnaissance Battalion. The Corps Order of the Day listed 10,000 prisoners, 159 guns, fifty-six tanks and two armoured trains among the booty.

The inevitable counter-attacks came in; waves of tanks and infantry from three separate divisions thrusting into the gaps in the German line. It would, perhaps, be more accurate to write of individual strongpoints, for the diary records: 'It is not possible in words to describe winter on this front. There is no main battle line, no outposts, no reserves. Just small groups of us depending upon each other to hold defended points . . . We are in the sunny South, how frightful must it be for the comrades up North. Here life is paralysed . . . you would never believe the lavatory procedures . . . And the food . . . we live on a sort of thick soup made of ground buckwheat and millet. We have to strip the fallen, theirs and ours, for warm clothing. I don't think I will ever be warm again and our tame Ivans say that this is a mild winter. God preserve us.'

With tanks and guns unusable through cold and with only their infantry weapons to defend themselves, without adequate clothing, in positions on the open steppe, sharing one cigarette among five men, without relief, outnumbered and isolated, the SS infantry held fast. Waves of Russians crossed the Don in furious assaults only to fall in a fury of killing. These battles were really fights for survival in its most primitive form, for a unit which was driven from its prepared positions was forced on to the naked steppe with the absolute necessity of finding or constructing some shelter from the Buran – the icy wind – before it killed them. 'They came in . . . in masses so great as to numb the senses. They had to pick their way through the dead of the other assaults who are still unburied. We drove them off – how easy it seems to write this . . . and when they had gone back across the ice the whole area to both flanks and in front of our positions was carpeted with dead. They were dead all right . . . the wounded die quickly; the blood freezes as it leaves the body and a sort of shock sets in which kills. Light wounds that heal in three days in summer kill you in the winter.'

The Army withdrew from Rostov, despite Hitler's initial order to fight to the last man. In the Führer's Headquarters, plans were being prepared for a resumption of the offensive by Army Group South to reach the Don–Donetz line; while in the combat zone the understrength SS Companies were battling to hold back successive waves of Siberian riflemen storming across the frozen waters of the river Mius.

A delayed but sincere Christmas greeting in respect of the Leibstandarte was the letter sent by von Mackensen, the Corps Commander, to the Reichsführer SS extolling Hitler's Guard for 'its discipline . . . it is refreshing to see the cheerfulness, energy and unshakeable steadfastness in time of crisis . . . a real élite unit . . .'

The severity of the winter of 1941–42 was sufficient to inhibit widespread military activity although operations did not stop altogether. During February a Russian offensive and local breakthrough near Dnieperpetrovsk brought III Corps out to seal off the breach and the Leibstandarte held the line while the German operation was being carried out. Then came the thaw and with the thaw came the mud. Once again the vehicles were bogged down. But by the beginning of May large-scale movement was beginning again. Führer Order N 41 made the South the decisive front and the task of Army Group South was to destroy the enemy in front of the Don, to cross the Caucasus and to seize the Caucasian oil-producing centres.

The opening of the summer offensive was delayed by a Russian spoiling attack which was launched on 12th May 1942, but a week later while German armoured pincers sealed off the Russian bridgehead south of Kharkov the Leibstandarte moved back to Stalino for refitting, reinforcement and retraining. During June the threat of another assault landing on the coast of France took the Leibstandarte from the command of Army Group South and brought it to the Western Front where it remained increasing in strength and status until its recall to Russia.

The first mission in Russia had been concluded and analysis of the first year shows that at the highest level Hitler had thrown away a strategic victory for tactical successes. Russian armies had been encircled and destroyed but the Red Army had escaped annihilation and had grown in strength and efficiency. Of the three German Army Groups only the South could claim that it had achieved its given objectives, and then only to a limited degree.

At all levels of SS command, but particularly at the lowest level of all, that of the simple SS soldier, the conviction was still firmly held that German organization, flexibility and professionalism were superior to the Russian. There was real respect for the Red Army soldier as an individual; there was a growing awareness of the vast resources of the Soviet Union and there was horror at the callousness of a political system that sacrificed troops in suicide attacks. The SS still saw the war with Russia as a crusade but by now they were not holding the line alone. Men of other European nations were enlisting and the SS ideas which had once been 'uniquely and proudly German became the inspiration of men of a dozen nations'.

The Leibstandarte had suffered terrible losses but it had gained for itself, as the other SS Divisions had gained for themselves, a reputation for *élan* in attack, for solidity in defence and a contempt for death which impressed the Army. The SS – the political soldiers – were becoming the model of those soldierly virtues which had once been the sole epitome of the Regular Army.

The Second Russian Campaign: January–August 1943

The period of the second campaign which the Leibstandarte fought in Russia covers the months January to August 1943, and includes such climactic battles as the loss and recapture of Kharkov and Operation 'Citadel', the Battle of Kursk, not only the greatest tank battle of all time, but also the last, major, German offensive on the Russian Front.

By the winter of 1942 the pattern of the war in Russia had taken on the motion of a pendulum, swinging eastwards with the German summer offensives and returning, westwards, as the Red Army fought its winter campaigns to regain lost territory. Only in the wet seasons of spring and autumn did movement halt, except for minor operations.

That part of the Soviet winter offensive of 1942 which struck at Army Group South destroyed the German Sixth Army at Stalingrad and through the gap, 200 miles wide, between Voronezh and Voroshilovgrad, Red armies were sweeping westwards towards the Dnieper. In the south Third Red Tank Army was driving forward on a line Poltava–Dnieperpetrovsk–Saporzhe to pin the Germans against the Black Sea and there to annihilate them. The advance of this and of other Red armies had bypassed Kharkov both to the north and south; despite supply difficulties and manpower shortages the momentum of the Soviet advance was still being maintained at the end of January 1943. The Soviet armoured spearheads were opening out, thereby offering open flanks to counter-blows, but the German Army was in no condition to strike back. Indeed only massive reinforcement would prevent a collapse of the whole southern wing.

On 9th January 1943, the SS Panzer Corps, comprising Leibstandarte, Das Reich and Totenkopf Divisions, was ordered to the Eastern Front with all possible speed. Given absolute rail and road priority the whole of the Adolf Hitler Division and the greater part of Das Reich were soon concentrated in Kharkov and then moved up the line; the Leibstandarte to take up a defensive position along the Donetz and Das Reich to hold advanced out-posts east of the river. The divisional sectors covered unusually long fronts; the Leibstandarte bridgehead at Chegevayev stretched for more than seventy miles and the thin line of Grenadiers defending the ground was reduced in number when Witt's Panzer Grenadier Regi-ment was ordered to Kubyansk to take part in a proposed Corps attack south-east of Alkatavka.

Against the storming tide of Russian attacks the remaining Leibstandarte regiments held the line, standing firm as rock while a confusion of retreating units, German, Italian and Hungarian, streamed westwards through the bridgehead. During the first week of February the Division's outposts were driven in, but in the blinding snowstorms which marked that week of battle Soviet assaults against the main defence line and particularly against the key bridgeheads position at Pechenege were smashed back with heavy loss by men prepared to die rather than break. Byelgorod, north of Kharkov, was evacuated and Das Reich Division withdrew to the Donetz, fighting every step of the way. But the units on either flank of the SS Corps had less fortitude and Soviet probing patrols found, at Smiyev, a forty-mile gap between the right flank of Leibstandarte and the left flank of 320th Infantry Division. The Corps concentrated an attack force to close this gap and thus avert the danger of the flank being turned. The first priority was to halt the Soviet advance. The capture of Merefa, a small town on Red Army's main road forward, would help accomplish this. The second task was to cut across the Red salient, to make contact with the main body of Army Group and to re-establish a continuous front line.

To carry out these operations a strong, composite battle group was set up, under Dietrich's command, and sent into the attack. In temperatures often 20 degrees below zero, heavily outnumbered and obstructed by deep snow-drifts, a three-pronged, armoured assault went in, preceded by Stuka dive-bombing attacks. The right arm was the Leibstandarte Reconnaissance Battalion. 'Der Führer' Regiment of Das Reich, together with the Leibstandarte Panzer Regiment, formed the centre column and Witt's 1st SS Panzer Grenadier Regiment constituted the left flank. Giant tasks demand more than normal efforts for their fulfilment and the achievements of the SS regiments in those days raised them in military esteem from being a crack unit to becoming the élite. Their courage and fighting ability gave the Leibstandarte men a moral superiority and the selfless behaviour of the officers inspired their men to greater efforts. It became common-place to see officers of senior field rank leading combat groups in all-out assaults. Becker, the Commander of No. 2 Company of 2nd SS Grenadier Regiment, led his men in hand-to-hand fighting for the village of Alexayevka,

and by midnight of 11th February it and Merefa had fallen
to the SS. During the morning of 12th February, Vodol-
oga Starekovka has been taken and 'Der Führer' Regiment captured Borki. For more than thirty miles the SS
columns drove across the Soviet spearhead severing it
completely and isolating VII Guard Cavalry Corps, but
Dietrich's Command was itself cut off from the main body
of the SS Corps.

Confused fighting took place as both sides fought for
supremacy; the Russians to maintain the tempo of their
offensive and the SS determined to halt the Soviet drive.

Ad hoc battle groups were formed as units were deci-
mated and combined with other SS Regiments to hold the
Donetz line. In the north the line was being forced back
on Kharkov. In other sectors village after village was torn
from SS control. Smiyev had gone; Ternovaya seemed
about to fall but at Rogan the SS were holding off
repeated and heavy assaults. The battle reached its crisis
during the night of 13th–14th February, and the last SS
reserves were put into action. Soviet advances had so
extended the Corps front that the line had become a
series of strongpoints and every able-bodied man was sent
in. Even the wounded went back to their units to help
hold off the Russian mass attacks. During this period of
strain one single incident of all that chronicle of battle
raised the spirits of the Corps, for it showed the character
of the SS at its best. The 320th Infantry Division, fighting
its way back to the main body of Army Group, was
surrounded and burdened with 1,500 wounded men whom
the divisional commander would not abandon to the
enemy. The Leibstandarte was asked to help. Peiper's SS
Panzer Grenadier Battalion crossed the Donetz below
Smiyev, penetrated more than twenty-five miles into
Soviet territory, smashed repeated counter-attacks and
then broke through to the hard-pressed infantry division.

The SS Battalion then formed a protective screen, and beating off infantry and tank assault convoyed the 320th back to the Donetz and saw them safely across. The river ice was too thin to bear the weight of Peiper's armoured vehicles so the column went back into Russian territory, cut a wide and destructive swathe through the Red Army's rear units and then regained the Leibstandarte positions.

Dietrich's battle group, completely isolated, was fighting a typical soldiers' battle on the drive south to link up with Fourth Panzer Army. At Bereka leading elements of the Reconnaissance Battalion, cut off from their armoured support, were desperately short of ammunition and fuel. Wünsche, commander of 1st Battalion of the SS Panzer Regiment, personally led the armoured group which broke through the Russian encirclement, and for this deed, as well as for his action in destroying fifty-four Russian guns and other equipment, received the Knight's Cross. Counter-attack followed attack as severe fighting continued for days in and around the villages and small towns which were taken, lost, retaken and then lost again. Bereka and Alexayevka changed hands frequently in the tides of battle and were surrounded by burnt-out vehicles, broken artillery pieces and the deep frozen dead. The Soviet armies although rebuffed were not defeated and, heavily reinforced, they stormed forward once again, this time with Kharkov as their immediate objective. The situation had reached the point where the German field commanders were insisting that a withdrawal from the town had to take place if the SS Panzer Corps was not to be trapped and destroyed. From Hitler's headquarters came the order to hold the town, and this uncompromising decision placed the SS leaders in a quandary. Were they to obey Hitler, to whom they had sworn unconditional obedience, or were they to save their men? Hausser, the SS Corps commander, ignored Hitler's direct order and decided to evacuate. He had little time, for the escape corridor to the west was no more than a mile wide and Red Army patrols had taken Ossnova, an eastern suburb. Peiper was sent in to recapture the town but even his dash proved unavailing. Early on the morning of 15th February, the first Red troops entered the south-eastern parts of Kharkov and by evening they were in the north-western sections of the town. The SS evacuated the town and withdrew behind the Uda river.

The slogging match in the south was still running its brutal course. On 16th February, a battalion of 'Der Führer' went in to break the ring around the Leibstandarte's armoured reconnaissance battalion and two days later 'Der Führer's' 3rd Battalion reinforced an assault carried out by Witt's regiment, which severe losses had now reduced to no more than a strong battalion. Tanarovka was reached, and while the main body of Leibstandarte fought defensive battles north of Krasnograd, 'Das Reich', having now covered sixty miles against fanatical resistance put up by Sixth Red Army, made contact with Fourth Panzer Army at Novo Moskovsk. The German front was sealed.

When Hausser visited the battle groups on 17th February, he brought happier news. A counter-attack was to be launched. The Corps would concentrate behind the Mscha river at Krasnograd ready to take part in Manstein's counter-offensive aimed at recapturing Kharkov. Although the fighting during the next days is classified as defensive many local minor and successful attacks such as the capture of Jerememkevka and of Nichni Orel were made during a spell of mild weather, a phenomenon of the Russian winter. Small-scale encirclements to snip off troublesome salients were carried out and attacks switched from flank to flank to bewilder the Russian command. When Pavlgorod fell to a fierce assault on 20th

February, the conditions for a successful counter-attack had been established.

The first part of Manstein's plan, to let the Russians come on and then to trap them in a pocket, was succeeding and by 21st February both First and Fourth Panzer Armies were positioned for the counter-stroke. The SS Panzer Corps, on Fourth Panzer Army's left flank, began its attack on the 22nd and three days later, fighting in a north-easterly direction, had captured Losowaya where it linked up with Army Panzer units coming from the west. The greater part of Popov's Armoured Corps was thereby encircled and then destroyed. The rapid and total destruction of the Russian group was aided by the employment of Corps artillery which fired on Popov's tanks at ranges exceeding 15,000 yards, destroying them utterly. Some Soviet units succeeded in breaking through the German encirclement by showing a complete disregard for losses but the greater part of First Guards Army and Popov's Group was smashed.

But the Soviets did not remain inactive and a counter-offensive by Third Guards Tank Army was anticipated. To put the Red Army off its stroke a spoiling attack was launched by the Leibstandarte, on 28th February, to capture a set of commanding heights east of the Bereka–Yefomevka road. The direction of the attack was then changed to threaten Valki, nearly a hundred miles to the east, and Totenkopf Division was brought into the line to close the flank. The three-day battle ended with the encirclement of XV Guards Armoured Corps. The preliminary stages were over and the German counter-offensive could begin. It opened well and ran its brilliant course. In the first days more than 600 tanks and over 1,000 guns were destroyed. On 4th March, an armoured assault by Leibstandarte rolled from Staroverovka. Behind the Mark IV point tanks came the heavy Tigers and, following them, the personnel carriers and then the armoured cars. In swift, fierce operations the enemy was surrounded and smashed.

By 6th March, a large number of major Soviet units had been cut off. The Corps thrust upon Valki then tore open the Russian defence lines. Through the gap poured the Leibstandarte, firstly to establish a bridgehead across the Mscha and then to widen it near Brdok. The clinging mud produced by the sudden thaw threatened to slow the advance but Weiser of No. 2 Motor Cycle Company of the SS Reconnaissance Battalion smashed the advance forward and Valki fell. Kharkov was the next objective. By 9th March the advance guard of Leibstandarte Division had reached Peretdinaga and Polevaya, forcing the Russians back across the Donetz. Now the all-out assault on Kharkov could begin.

Impatient to reconquer the city that had been evacuated on his command, Hausser launched two attacks, the one from the north and the second from the west. On 10th March, covered by Stuka assaults and supported by Nebelwerfer batteries, the SS Grenadiers went in, the Leibstandarte driving down from the north and the northwest. Witt's regiment put in a double-pronged assault with Hansen's 3rd SS Battalion in the van, and cut the Kharkov–Byelgorod road while Sandig's 2nd Battalion probed until it found a weak point in the Red line and drove it home. The Soviet forces in the city were trapped by the Leibstandarte units which raced to capture Red Square. Meyer's battalion gained the eastern edge of town by 11th March and cut the Staryi road but Russian counter-attacks against Witt's regiment in the Red Square sector involved the SS Grenadiers in house-to-house, often room-to-room battles which lasted for three days. Late in the afternoon of 15th March, the last Soviet resistance in the tractor factory ended and Kharkov had been recaptured. '. . . how pleased we all are with our success . . . we have thrown them back and Kharkov is German once again. We have shown the Ivans that we can withstand their terrible winter. It can hold no fear for us again . . .'

With the city firmly held Peiper was sent northwards and reached the Donetz, on 18th March, at Byelgorod. There he linked up with the 'Grossdeutschland' Division. The four-week counter-offensive was over; the objective to restore the line had been achieved and the German Army stood, once again, on the ground which it had conquered in 1942.

A German military commentator analysing the Russian winter offensive and the German counter-blow drew the conclusion that, despite a numerical superiority of 8:1 in infantry and of 5:1 in tanks, as well as in conditions which favoured them, the Soviet Army had been halted and driven back. The severity of the Soviet reverse was attributed to the inflexibility of the Red Army mind and the inability at all levels of command to switch from a victorious advance to the bitterness of retreat. The panic routs which occurred throughout the period of the German counter-attack, and particularly in the Popov group, were evidences of this instability.

To the SS Corps the price of their victory was the loss of 365 officers and 11,154 other ranks in dead, wounded and missing covering the period from January to 18th March.

The front then went into a period of relative calm and the Leibstandarte on to security duties in and around Kharkov.

Operation 'Citadel': The Battle of Kursk

The Soviet winter offensive of 1942–43 had been halted and flung back but the effort which had been required emphasized the serious shortage of manpower from which Germany was suffering. Losses which had amounted to 922,000 casualties by the end of 1942 (a proportion of 14.2 per cent) rose by the end of 1943 to 2,033,000 casualties (a proportion of 30.6 per cent). The strength of the Army declined to three million men, and the Supreme Command's demand for three-quarters of a million men produced only a quarter of that number. This meant, quite simply, that future losses would never be replaced in full and that the German Army would steadily decrease in numbers. On the industrial front German tank production was incapable of supplying a full establishment of armoured vehicles to the Panzer divisions, whereas Russian production had risen to 1,000 machines per month, sufficient for both replacement and expansion.

The long-term question to be decided was whether future military operations on the Eastern Front were to be totally defensive, or whether the Army should seek to maintain the military initiative and, by mounting local attacks, to bleed the Russian Army to death. Meanwhile a more immediate problem needed to be resolved. A huge and powerful Russian salient, over 400 miles long and 150 miles deep, left over from the winter campaign, was threatening the right flank of Army Group Centre and Army Group South's left wing. The Supreme Command Chief of Staff pressed for an offensive to pinch out the Kursk salient at the earliest possible date. Ideally, had it been possible, the spring counter-offensive should have been continued until the line had been straightened, but, better late than never, orders were given for the attack to take place.

Operation 'Citadel' was planned and a build-up of troops began. The intention was to mass and launch two armoured forces; the northern arm, furnished by Army Group Centre, would meet the southern arm of Army

Group South and within the pincers the encircled Soviet armies would be destroyed. The main burden of the southern attack was to be borne by Fourth Panzer Army, massed west of Byelgorod, which had been given the task of breaking through the Soviet positions on both sides of Konarovka and driving, via Oboyan, to attain the objective, Kursk.

The plan was by no means accepted unanimously. Within the Supreme Command there were dissident voices which protested at the folly of hazarding the whole of Germany's military future on one strategically unimportant operation. Hitler himself confessed to having his stomach turn over at the thought and, in his indecision, postponed D-Day from 1st May to a succession of other dates before finally deciding on 5th July. This delay favoured the Soviets and gave them the time to construct a deep, well-armed system of fortifications protected by extensive minefields and the impressive growth rate of Red Army strength (6,000 armoured fighting vehicles had been delivered to the Soviet armies by the end of June) left the Russians confident of victory. The Soviet High Command was determined to destroy the offensive power of the German Army and had selected Kursk to be the battlefield upon which it would attain the military dominance. It is true to say that the Red Army commanders viewed the forthcoming battle as a new Verdun.

Throughout the early months of the summer of 1943 German assault divisions practised battle drills and tactics. The two most favoured armoured tactics were the wedge and the bell. The first penetrated the enemy line and then smashed open the breach using Tiger tanks, whose armour was proof against Russian anti-tank guns, as the point of the wedge. The bell tactic was that of massive penetration at two points and the crushing of the enemy line within those points. The clapper of the bell was the

Division Command Group, which could move from flank to flank across the bell mouth. The swiftly changing pattern of armoured battles had always required that senior commanders be well forward; for Operation 'Citadel' it was vital that tight and immediate control be up with the leading tanks.

The Red Army's defensive tactic against the German Panzers was an adaptation of the German Pakfront, a solid block of anti-tank guns whose massed punch could be directed upon individual and selected targets. The clever siting of minefields would channel the Panzers on to the massed guns of the Pakfront. But the Soviet plan was not all defensive and tank patrols would seal off local German advances until the time came for the final blow which would sweep the Germans from the field. The 115 divisions of the Red Army massed in the salient around Kursk stood confident and secure behind belts of fortifications eight miles deep.

The battlefield was a huge plain, an agricultural region covered either with corn or by belts of tall, steppe grass and broken by valleys, small hills, and by several watercourses of which the Donetz, the Pena, Psel and Seyn were the most important. The sand roads turned to mud tracks in heavy rain. Tactically the ground favoured the Soviets for the plain rose gently towards Kursk, giving the Russians complete observation.

The Fourth Panzer Army, with ten divisions under command, was the stronger of the two Panzer armies, one with each Army Group, chosen for Operation 'Citadel'. Its total strength in tanks and self-propelled guns was 1,137, of which no less than 200 tanks were Panthers, eighty-one were Tigers and the remainder Marks III or IV.

The task of the SS Panzer Corps, part of Fourth Panzer Army, was to advance via Beresov and Sadeynoye, thus penetrating the first defensive belt. Between Lutchki and

Jakovlevo was the second line of fortifications and when these were smashed the advance would follow in a generally north-eastern direction. For this operation 167th Infantry Division would form part of the SS Corps and would guard the left flank. As D-Day drew near, the SS Corps, with a strength of 343 tanks and 195 SP guns, moved forward into its pre-battle observation and jump-off positions. The Grenadiers and the commanders were confident. Everything had been prepared. They could not fail; they must not fail; too much depended upon their efforts. 'For reasons of security we have not been allowed to move about during the daytime and you can understand how hard this is, but now the waiting is over . . . it is coal black outside the Command bunker. Black clouds cover the sky and the rain is streaming down. We are rested and refreshed . . . the mud might slow us down but it cannot stop us. Nothing will. The barrage has just begun. I can feel its force even down here deep in the earth.'

Dawn of the morning of 5th July 1943, the first day of Operation 'Citadel', heralded a six-hour-long battle during which the Russian bunker line was penetrated. At 03.45 hours the Stukas began dive-bombing attacks supplementing the artillery barrage which had been poured on Byelgorod and fifteen minutes later the Tiger tanks of the armoured wedge rolled forward; the Battle for Kursk had begun, the so-called 'Death Ride of the Fourth Panzer Army', was under way. 'I saw our leading Tiger sections roar away and vanish almost completely in the peculiar silver/grey tall grass which is a feature of the area . . . Our mine-lifting teams mark the position of Ivan's mines by lying down alongside them, thus using their bodies to mark a gap in the field. There are thousands of mines all over the area . . .'

The Leibstandarte advance began with practised ease, the tank squadrons encircling an enemy who would then be wiped out by the supporting Grenadiers. The rhythm of the advance was exhilarating and the first defensive positions were overrun without difficulty, but in the face of massed, heavy Russian artillery and extensive minefields the impetus slowed and then halted between the first and second lines. Now was the moment when the quality of SS leadership began to tell. Karck, commanding 9th Company of the Leibstandarte's 2nd SS Panzer Grenadier Regiment, led his men into a dashing assault to capture two hills west of Byelgorod and personally destroyed five Soviet fortified positions with explosive charges. For as long as the operation continued examples of heroism by Grenadiers and by tank-men show this determination for victory in attack and doggedness in defence against overwhelming odds. The tank-men, too, went all out to achieve the breakthrough. Wittmann, with whom the Kursk operation is completely identified, destroyed on this first day eight of a total of thirty tanks he was to claim before the battle ended, as well as twenty-eight anti-tank guns knocked out and two battalions of infantry cut up and dispersed. Quite soon the Red Army began flinging in counter-attacks, using squadrons of tanks against single German machines and guns. During the fighting around the Stalinsk Kolkhoz no less than forty Soviet armoured vehicles attacked Samtreiter's platoon of four anti-tank guns and lost twenty-four of their number before the others drew off to allow a two-battalion assault of Soviet infantry against this small Leibstandarte unit. When the last round of anti-tank ammunition had been fired Samtreiter led his men into an infantry-type battle smashing back the Red Army penetrations. This first day's fighting was to cost the Leibstandarte 97 killed and 522 wounded.

Bad weather on 6th July postponed the Leibstandarte thrust until the afternoon and when the attack did go in the SS tank-men and Grenadiers encountered the dug-in tanks of Vatutin's First Red Tank Army, flame throwers and constant counter-attacks. The Soviets had mobilized every person they could reach and partisan activity in the Corps rear area had to be subdued in a series of small actions. Instances were recorded of Red Army battalions made up of civilians, without uniforms, many without boots and most without weapons, but all put into attacks as part of the 'human wave' tactic. Two reports mention all-women battalions fighting as savagely as the Soviet men. The Red Army was relying on mass to smother the thin line of German infantry. Again the Leibstandarte's losses were heavy – 84 killed and 384 wounded.

The High Command War Diary for 6th July commented that the element of surprise had not been achieved and, although noting a twelve-mile advance on that day and recording the fighting during the 7th in the enemy's second position, indicated that no decisive breakthrough had occurred. Both flanks of the SS Corps were now open to Russian counterblows, for XXXXVIII Panzer Corps on the left flank had failed to keep abreast of the SS while the right flank unit had progressed very little at all during the two days of battle. The War Diary for 8th July claimed the destruction, by that date, of 400 Russian tanks and indeed losses on both sides had been high. By the end of D-Day plus three the Corps had only forty Panther tanks still operational of the 200 which had entered upon the battle. 'Some baled-out crews came into our trenches for safety . . . they do not trust their machines and they say that a hit often causes a fire so that the machines blaze like torches. Some of the crews are very new and inexperienced. For some this is their first battle . . .' Other faults came to light. The Ferdinands, super heavy tank destroyer Tigers with tremendous thicknesses of armour, suffered from weaknesses in the suspension and were frequently immobilized, and the remote-controlled, unmanned, demolition tanks 'Goliath' proved impotent to destroy the Soviet fortifications. These defensive positions stopped the German attack almost completely and the Leibstandarte assault, although maintaining a forward movement, had no rhythm. The strain of battle exhausted everyone. The Grenadiers slept where they dropped and the tank crews, half dead from noise and fumes, stretched out by their machines smothered in a deep sleep from which not even the noise of the maintenance and servicing crews could wake them.

The battle orders for the Leibstandarte on 7th July named Oboyan and Teterevino as the immediate objectives and the tank battalions roared into battle under the supporting bombardment of Luftwaffe bombers. Wittmann increased his score by knocking out seven more T34s as well as nineteen guns of the Red 29th Anti-tank Brigade. A Leibstandarte motor-cycle company, roaring through a gap created by Wittmann, captured intact a Russian Brigade headquarters and by this constant pressure the SS Panzers and Grenadiers drove the advance forward to Psyolknee. There the Russian counter-blow came in against No. 13 Company of 1st SS Panzer Regiment and almost exclusively against Staudegger and his Tiger tank. The Soviets tried hard to break through but, in a battle which endured for more than two hours, Staudegger and his crew destroyed more than twenty of the fifty T34s which had begun the assault and drove off the remainder.

The high claims made by SS tank crews during the Russian campaign and specifically during Operation 'Citadel' seem by Western experience to be wildly exaggerated, but the West is unfamiliar with the Soviet tactic of mass and the prodigal waste of lives and machines to gain objectives. Comparisons show that the 'kill' claims put in by Army units are on a par with the SS while claims by Luftwaffe pilots of their victories are also numbered in hundreds. It is probable that the Leibstandarte put out of action some 500 Soviet tanks in the nine days up to 14th July.

During the bitter fighting which marked the passage of those July days, 2nd Battalion 1st SS Panzer Regiment, commanded by Gross, claimed no less than ninety Soviet tanks destroyed in three hours, and von Ribbentrop, son of the German Foreign Minister, knocked out six of the forty Russian tanks which he had ambushed at Teterevino. Three days later, on 12th July, his No. 6 Company of 1st SS Panzer Regiment was attacked by 154 T34s and an infantry battalion advancing between Prokorovka and Teterevino. Fighting at ranges which frequently reduced to under 200 yards Ribbentrop's troop, reduced from seven machines to only four, fought on and destroyed the enemy attacks. His personal claim for that day was fourteen Red tanks. Wittmann, moving his Tiger troop forward in support of a Grenadier assault, encountered and drove off the attack by sixty Soviet tanks and then smashed another attack by 181 Red Tank Brigade, destroying that unit utterly as a fighting formation. The professionalism and technical ability of the SS was often sufficient to turn the balance even when the Russians had overwhelming superiority in numbers and the sheer courage of the Leibstandarte officers brought the attacks forward. Peiper's 3rd SS Panzer Grenadier Battalion, fighting on the Red Heights near Byelgorod, came under attack by Soviet tank units which roared in behind a heavy and damaging bombardment. Picking his moment with care Peiper destroyed one T34 in close combat and his adjutant Wolff, not to be outdone, then led a group of SS Grenadiers in a tank hunting and destroying mission, halting the breakthrough attempt.

On 10th July the commander of the Soviet Voronezh Front, with a force of 10 Corps under command, went over to the counter-offensive and launched his tank columns against those of Army Group South. On the plain to the south of Kursk two mighty tank armies deployed for the decisive battle. The massive blows by the Soviet tank armies struck most violently against the SS and III Corps. By evening knocked-out tanks of both nations littered the steppes and smoke from burning machines darkened the skies above the salient. The High Command War Diary recorded the destruction of 663 Soviet tanks, and although it is true that Russian losses far exceeded the German, theirs could be made good; German losses, except where the tanks could be recovered, were total. Against increasingly heavy Soviet tank thrusts the advance by the southern pincer arm began to slow down; the northern arm had been stationary for days. The War Diary recorded the fact that Fourth Panzer Army had established bridgeheads across the Donetz and again that slight gains in ground were still being made. It was, however, patently clear that 'Citadel' would never attain the objectives which had been expected and by 19th July further attacks were cancelled. Withdrawals to shorten the line were approved. It was all over.

The last major German offensive in Russia had faded. Army Group South lost 20,700 men (3,300 of whom were killed). Army Group Centre's Ninth Army lost over 10,000 men in two days. Infantry divisions had shrunk to the level of regiments and Panzer divisions to that of armoured battalions. The actual strength of the SS Panzer Corps on 16th July was thirty Mark VI, sixty-nine Mark IV, eighty Mark III and four Mark II tanks. There were, in addition, twenty Command vehicles, eleven captured T34s and sixty-four self-propelled guns.

Opposite above: The Motor-Cycle Reconnaissance Detachment of the Leibstandarte on a mountain road in the Peloponnese.

Opposite below: A 15cm field howitzer of the Leibstandarte in action in the Klissura Pass. Greece, 1941.

Right: 'Sepp' Dietrich, the first commander and creator of the Leibstandarte, of whom Hitler said 'he is a national institution'.

Below: A 3.7cm anti-tank gun (Pak) in action. Russia, 1941.

Left: A captured tank-man of the Red Army being interrogated by SS Field Police of the Leibstandarte Division.

Right: Panzer Grenadiers resting during the advance in the summer of 1942.

Left: SS Panzer Grenadiers of the Leibstandarte Division awaiting orders to move forward. Russia, 1942.

Right: The Leibstandarte's Tank Regiment preparing to move forward. Russia, 1943.

Above: The Leibstandarte in Kharkhov, 1943. SS Standarterführer Witt alongside an armoured personne carrier Sd.Kfz 251.

Left: SS Obersturmführer Rudolf von Ribbentrop, son of the German Foreign Minister, who was awarded the Knight's Cross of the Iron Cross on 17th July 1943 at the age of 22. He was at that time commanding No. 6 Company of 1st SS Panzer Regiment

Opposite above: SS Panzer Grenadiers moving into the attack during the summer battles of 1943.

Opposite below: A Mark IV moving through a French village, 1944, just before making contact with the Allied forces.

Left: A machine-gun group pauses for a smoke during the Ardennes offensive.

Below: A Leibstandarte Panzer Grenadier in the Ardennes, 1944. He is wearing the summer field service jacket and is carrying the Assault Pistol 44.

Opposite above: Men of Peiper's Battle Group on the Malmédy road during the Ardennes, 1944.

Opposite below: Leibstandarte soldiers enjoying American PX supplies. Ardennes, 1944.

Above: A young Leibstandarte man taken by soldiers of the US Army. December 1944.

Left: SS Sturmbannführer Hansen in Hungary, 1945.

The Soviets had harnessed the Panzer storm-wind and had gained control over the conduct of military affairs, which they were never to lose. The Red Army price for this victory was 2,108 tanks, 190 guns and 33,000 prisoners. The numbers of Soviet dead are unknown.

On 20th July Russian attacks began against the Bryansk–Orel railway and the Leibstandarte, re-organizing and refitting in the Isyum area, re-entered the battle along the Mius river line. The division was withdrawn on 3rd August and posted to Italy where the Fascist régime of Benito Mussolini had collapsed as a consequence of the Allied invasion of Sicily. A strong, tough and politically reliable German division was needed in Italy to prevent the whole peninsula from falling into the hands of the Western Allies and Hitler decided that his Leibstandarte was the one unit which had the required potential. For the next three months the men of the Leibstandarte spent the time as Occupation Forces engaging, from time to time, in anti-partisan operations in northern Italy and in Slovenia.

The Third Russian Campaign: November 1943 to April 1944

As a consequence of the failure of Operation 'Citadel', the German Army in Russia ceased to be the hammer and became instead the anvil. Now it was the German Army which was on the defensive and those towns which, during 1941 and 1942, had been milestones on a highway to victory were, in 1944, stages on the bitter road to defeat.

The imposing strength of forty-two divisions under command of Army Group South did not reflect a true picture, for the infantry component of most of them was less than a sixth of the establishment and for some of them the divisional strength in rifles was only a thousand. In armour, too, the Army Group was seriously under strength for it had a total of only eighty-three tanks and ninety-eight self-propelled guns. Against this force the Red Army could muster sufficient infantry, tank, motorized and cavalry corps to give it a majority of 7:1 overall and of 40:1 at selected points.

The Soviets, confident in their superiority, were repeating as a summer offensive the strategic plan of winter 1942. Rapid advances captured Kharkov and with only a short halt, caused more by logistical difficulties than by the German defence, had continued until – by the last quarter of 1943 – Saporzhe, Melitopol and Kiev had all fallen. Ignoring, bypassing or outflanking German counter-attacks the Red Army swept on and it seemed as if the destruction of Army Group South was about to be realized. It was against this dark background that the Leibstandarte, together with other divisions, was recalled to the East. Order, counter-order, disorder had the SS Panzer Division struggling to assemble and reroute its units which had been detrained in First Panzer Army sector and which had then been posted to XXXXVIII Corps of Fourth Panzer Army. This army was located in an arc south of Kiev and the Leibstandarte, one of the seven divisions of XXXXVIII Corps, took up positions between the right and centre corps.

The first task of the Fourth Panzer Army was to strengthen the Army Group's northern wing, then it was to close the gap in the line and to attack the flank of Thirty-eighth Red Army by striking towards Zhitomir. Finally, it was to smash the Soviet bridgehead on the west bank of the Dnieper.

The XXXXVIII Corps was to attack north-westwards from Fastov to capture Zhitomir and to cut the Soviet supply routes by road and rail between Kiev and Zhitomir.

The Leibstandarte was to be the main attacking division and was to strike northwards with the Army's 1st Panzer Division on its left flank.

Not all the German divisions had arrived on the field of battle when the attack opened on 13th November but the offensive was not delayed and the missing elements were put straight into combat as they reached their positions. The Leibstandarte formed two battle groups. The left arm went via Rogosna, crossed the Kamenka and Unova rivers and cut the Fastov–Brodel railway line south of Mochnachka. The right group drove north-eastwards, passed Pistachki, captured Trylissi, threw bridgeheads across the Kamenka river and pushed towards Fastov. Both groups then halted; one to drive back the Soviet counter-attacks in the Mochnachka area while the other guarded the flank north-east of Komuty as the 1st, 7th and 8th Panzer Divisions fought for Zhitomir. It fell to them on 19th November. The Leibstandarte then turned east towards Brusilov, a town north-east of Fastov. It was here that the first major tank battles of the offensive were fought and Wittmann, whose star had been rising since well before 'Citadel', came into his own as, probably, the greatest tank fighter of the Second World War. On one November morning he destroyed six Russian tanks and five anti-tank guns before driving to the rear echelon to refuel and to take on more ammunition. Returning to the battle after lunch he then destroyed a further ten tanks and another seven guns. Reitlinger of the SS Self-Propelled Gun Battalion's No. 3 Company also demonstrated the ability of the Leibstandarte men. Sent out on reconnaissance he discovered thirty enemy armoured vehicles and went immediately into the attack, destroyed six of them and drove off the others, thus enabling the SS Grenadiers to reach the Kiev–Zhitomir highway. Brusilov then fell and the SS advance was continued as a single column. From Mochnachka it went through the wooded country of that region, crossed the Irpen river and had reached Divin by 26th November. Defensive positions were then taken up by one group which concentrated north of Chomutets and by the other north-east of Vilshke, both groups battling hard against the Russian cavalry, infantry and armoured assaults.

The Germans had succeeded in halting the Red advance for the appearance on the battlefield of fresh, abundantly equipped, élite divisions confounded the Russian troops and they broke under the assault. But their High Command reacted firmly; established a bridgehead at Cherkassy and launched firstly the 1st, and then 1st, 5th and 8th Guards Tank Corps against XXXXVIII Corps. The German Commander planned to encircle the Russian units but the Leibstandarte attack, which had set off in pouring rain, was smashed with heavy loss and the other divisions of Corps had as little success against the strongly entrenched enemy. Confused and bitter fighting took place but slowly the great combat experience of the German units realized the Corps plan. Peiper, now commanding the Leibstandarte's SS Panzer Regiment, broke through the Russian front and captured the staffs of four divisions. He then went on to make a twenty-six-mile-deep penetration during which he overran whole batteries of Russian field artillery and Pakfronts. Peiper's successes in this fighting amounted to over 100 tanks destroyed as well as seventy-six anti-tank guns and other *matériel*. The spearheads of the two 1st Panzer Divisions, that of the Army and that of the SS, closed behind the Soviets and although many Russians fought their way out of encirclement, 153 tanks, 70 pieces of artillery, and 250 anti-tank guns were destroyed and thousands of prisoners taken.

The Soviets reinforced the troops holding the Kiev road and the counter-attacks against the advancing Germans became stronger. Inevitably the Panzer thrusts slowed down and then halted. It was clear that the German High Command plan had been too ambitious and that the Dnieper bridgehead could not be reduced. Operations ceased on 23rd November, when warm weather turned the roads into mud tracks, and Fourth Panzer Army halted on a line running from Fastov to Korosten.

The offensive had achieved certain objectives. It had driven back the Soviets in such confusion that the Red Army Command had had to draw tank and mobile troops from other sectors and, on a material plane, it had, according to the High Command communiqué, taken 4,800 Red Army men prisoner, killed a further 20,000 and destroyed 603 tanks as well as 1,305 guns.

But these losses did not halt completely the Red Army's advance and in desperate fighting the troops of the First Ukrainian Front renewed the attack upon the Fourth Panzer Army. Manstein had anticipated this and had regrouped his forces to bar the way west. On 4th December the XXXXVIII Corps was moved to an attack position north of Zhitomir from which it could launch its own assaults against those units of Sixtieth Red Army which had not been hit during the November battles. It was then to drive on to the Teterev river at a point north of Radomischl. The battle opened with Wittmann's Tigers advancing against the Russian positions, protected by a series of mutually supporting Pakfronts. Wittmann fought fire with fire and concentrated the guns of his tanks against the massed artillery of the Pakfronts, destroying them one after the other. When the Tiger group reached this main highway to Styrty it was seen to be full with convoys of soft-skinned vehicles with tank and SP escort. The columns were attacked, left blazing and wrecked. The SS

Panzers then pushed the advance to the village of Golovin where another tank battle took place during which Wittmann destroyed his sixtieth victim. At dawn on 7th December the Leibstandarte, on Corps right flank, moved out of its concentration area north-west of Chernyakov and attacked eastwards, smashing the Soviet defence so thoroughly that Styrty was captured within four hours. The SS advance then skirted south of Korchevka, cut the Golubovka road, captured Torchin and headed north-eastwards towards Sabolot. For the next week the fighting continued and only slight progress was made. Blinding snowstorms, intense cold and savage counter-attacks by an enemy who was constantly and massively reinforced reduced the pace of the advance. By this period of the war the Luftwaffe had been withdrawn to fight the Allied bombing offensive and the Red Air Force had complete mastery of the air. But against all these obstacles the Leibstandarte pushed forward until, by 13th December, the Soviets had been forced back to the eastern bank of the Teterev river. Quickly the SS pressed the advantage home and the advance was continued, on the following day, east from Vishtshevitchi towards Vyrva. In the afternoon orders came withdrawing the SS Division from the line and posting it northwards. High Command had seen the chance to encircle the whole Sixtieth Red Army which was renewing its offensive against Zhitomir. The divisions of Fourth Panzer Army, weakened by nearly five weeks' campaigning, were expected to encircle forty-seven infantry and nine tank divisions of the Red Army. The plan was for a thrust against the Soviet northern flank to be followed by an encirclement, the jaws of which were to meet around Malin.

On 18th December, thirty artillery batteries and a number of Nebelwerfer units helped to lift the Leibstandarte attack across the Korosten–Chernyakov road and to carry it forward until it had cut the railway line and captured Turchinka. In the heavily wooded country outside the town the pace of the advance slowed as the SS Panzer Grenadier battalions were drawn into fighting a conventional infantry-type war against an enemy well dug in and superior in numbers. But the drive continued in a north-easterly direction. Bridgeheads were forced across the Trostyvitsa and, hanging the division's flank on the east bank of that river, the Leibstandarte then swung towards Peregorch at the confluence of the Trostyvitsa and Irsha rivers. The place was reached on 19th December.

For the next two days the Leibstandarte fought hard to hold the gains it had made. The SS units were subjected to intense bombardments by whole divisions of artillery, used as a variant of the Pakfront, to destroy utterly and swiftly any German opposition. Difficulties of terrain hindered communications between the SS units while allowing Russian infiltration. In the south-western sector the Leibstandarte line was forced back but the situation was eased on the northern flank when the SS sent twenty-five of its Tigers into a joint raid with a Panzer Grenadier regiment of 1st Panzer Division. The combined armoured group drove its way into a Soviet tank concentration area north of Shevshentka and smashed it.

A short-lived wave of optimism then swept through the soldiers of Army Group South. The Red Army prisoners who had been taken during the offensive had been either very young boys or old men and the hope grew that, at last, the Soviets had begun to exhaust their vast reserves of manpower and that the war might yet be fought on approximately equal terms.

On Christmas Eve, the last it was to spend fighting in Russia, the Leibstandarte and the rest of XXXXVIII Corps attacked south-eastwards to gain touch with 8th

Panzer Division and then to swing south to attack the
strong Soviet tank groups moving towards the
north–south Highway. During the fighting around and
along that road Wendorff, a platoon commander in the
Heavy Tank Company, rescued SS Panzer Grenadier
units which had been cut off, smashed twelve T34s during
one day's fighting and a further eleven of a group of
twenty which attacked him on the next day. Soon the
Corps was in position protecting Berdichev, south of
Zhitomir, against Soviet attacks. The full force of the re-
opened Russian winter offensive smashed against Fourth
Panzer Army and broke a twenty-mile gap in the line.
Manstein's regrouping moves sent the XXXXVIII Corps
to protect the flank and to prevent a breakthrough into
the rear of Panzer Army. On 6th January, 1944, Vatutin's
columns of Soviet tanks were striking southwards towards
the Dnieper bend, ignoring the Panzer Corps which
blocked his way. Not that their opposition could have
been very effective for the rifle strength of most divisions
had now shrunk to less than two hundred men. On the
northern flank other Soviet forces in the area of the Pripet
Marshes opened a new offensive; the whole southern
front was embattled.

During the course of this heavy defensive fighting
Wittmann once again proved his capacity when on 9th
January his group of three Tigers was sent on a reconnaissance mission. In a wadi a Russian tank group was
surprised and destroyed, six of the ten victims falling to
the 8.8cm gun of Wittmann's Tiger.

Five days later on the afternoon of 14th January
brought the crisis of the battle. A mass of Russian
armoured vehicles, T34s and Klementi Voroshilovs came
rolling down upon the German positions. Wittmann's
group moved to meet the charge. For hours the fighting
went on in bitter cold and poor visibility, but at the end

of the morning Wittmann alone had smashed sixteen Red tanks, and by the end of the day a further three tanks and three super-heavy SP guns had fallen to him. The Leibstandarte was fighting the battle of its life. Kling, commander of the Heavy Tank Company, led his men to achieve the destruction of 343 Soviet tanks, 8 assault guns and 225 heavy anti-tank guns during the fighting around Zhitomir, Korosten and Berdichev. On 12th January alone the Leibstandarte destroyed twenty T34s and, on the following day, it smashed a further twenty-seven Russian tanks. On the sector held by the Leibstandarte the Soviets were paying a high price for their advances.

To close the gap in Fourth Panzer Army's line Manstein moved First Panzer Army to the Uman–Vinnitsa sector and the Leibstandarte was posted to XXXXVI Panzer Corps of that Army. On 24th January the SS Division spearheaded an attack from the Vinnitsa area against First Red Tank Army which had crossed the Bug river. Although the opening stages of the battle were successful the Soviets put in an encircling move by a Guards tank army and a motorized army. Against these fresh, heavily armed opponents even the *élan* of the Leibstandarte could not prevail. But then, on 28th January, came the chance for First Panzer Army to carry out its own envelopment against the Soviet pincers. The XXXXVI and the III Corps cast a net which trapped several of the Red Army divisions. More than 700 tanks and self-propelled guns as well as 8,000 prisoners were taken.

But on the same day, on another sector of the Army Group Front, a Soviet advance in the Cherkassy region had trapped 50,000 Germans around Svenegordka and requests to allow these divisions to break out were refused by Hitler who demanded that the Dnieper line be held at all costs. Elaborate plans were drawn up for a breakthrough to be followed by a defeat of the encircling

Russian divisions, concluding with the recapture of Kiev. On one wing the XXXXVI Panzer Corps, with five armoured divisions, and III Panzer Corps, with four Panzer divisions, forming the other wing, were to strike deep into the enemy rear. Once contact had been made with the encircled troops then the two attacking corps were to turn inwards, trapping the Fourth and Fifth Guards Armies, Twenty-seventh, Fifty-second and Fifty-third Red Armies and V Guards Cavalry Corps.

A sudden thaw produced the Rasputitsa, the thigh-deep mud of the Ukraine, hindering the concentration of III Corps' four divisions, which were, in any case, deeply involved in fighting to disengage themselves from the Soviets. By D-Day for the operation, 3rd February 1944, only 16th and 17th Panzer Divisions were in position and the opening date was postponed for twenty-four hours.

Meanwhile the troops inside the Cherkassy pocket, subjected to continual Soviet assaults on their flanks, were suddenly faced with a new series of frontal attacks by troops of Third and Fourth Ukrainian Fronts. To the trapped men the fact that the escape plans were beautifully drawn up was little consolation: their need was to be rescued. Their practical views were sound, for the attack northwards by III Corps had little military value. Firstly, the direction of the advance was wrong, for the Cherkassy pocket lay to the east. Secondly, only a handful of German divisions was set to attack five Red armies and even if the advance did reach Medvin or Boyarka then the Soviets would cut it off to form a new and isolated pocket. But in obedience to orders the offensive began. Even before the attack could develop the effort by two Panzer and two infantry divisions had stuck fast in the deep mud.

When 1st Panzer and the Leibstandarte Divisions arrived in the field they were put straight into the attack to revive it and to bring it forward. This they succeeded in doing so that by 8th February elements of the SS and of 16th Panzer Divisions had reached and established bridgeheads across the Gniloi Tickich river, west of Boyarka. Wittmann played a significant part in these assaults and on 8th February took eleven Tiger tanks on a patrol during which he destroyed a further nine T34s. Two days later eighteen Soviet SP guns lay in ambush for the SS tank-man but he evaded the trap and destroyed thirteen of the vehicles. Other Tigers of his platoon accounted for the remaining Soviet machines. His score had now reached 107 enemy machines destroyed.

The drive of men like Wittmann brought the Leibstandarte attack forward until the armoured wedge was more than twenty miles deep inside the Soviet front – but the drive was still heading in the wrong direction. At last came the order changing the direction eastwards and III Corps regrouped for the final twenty miles of fighting which would break through to the encircled divisions. The SS withdrew its bridgehead across the Gniloi Tickich and prepared for the advance that was to thrust via Ninograd, to pass south of Boyarka, through Bushanka and Lysanka to reach Kvitky.

The attack went in on 11th February, over ground which a frost had hardened sufficiently to take the heavy tanks. The Leibstandarte, grouped with 16th and 17th Panzer Divisions, made up the northern flank while 1st Panzer Division formed the southern. The Soviet High Command had not anticipated the German change of direction and was thrown off balance, but quickly recovered and put V Guards Armoured Corps against the Panzers. The Red Guard counter-thrust cut off the German relief force but the pace of the attack continued although more and more vehicles were dropping out due to the appalling weather and road conditions. Behind the

German armour, Red infantry seeped back separating the tank spearheads from the follow-up Grenadier units. The single co-ordinated drive was deteriorating into a series of bitter little battles along the escape corridor. Against the Leibstandarte's extended northern flank the Soviets then flung the full weight of XVI Red Tank Corps, forcing the SS to give ground. The 17th Panzer Division came up in support, leaving only 16th Panzer to continue the assault. On 13th February the spearheads of that division came under acute pressure and the attack faltered, then stopped with only eight miles separating the Panzer spearheads from the encircled troops. Exhausted by their efforts the relief Corps halted on the line Lysanka–Oktyar–Chisinzy.

While the Leibstandarte and the Army Panzer divisions had been fighting their bitter way forward, Hitler, at last, consented to the evacuation of the Cherkassy pocket. The elaborate breakout plans proved to be unworkable in practice and chaos resulted from their failure. The SS 'Das Reich' Division was among the rearguard units in the pocket, holding fast while the bulk of the encircled troops made good their escape. Some days later, seen only dimly through the murk of the February overcast, men of the Leibstandarte outposts saw a slow-moving procession dragging itself through the waist-high snow. It was some of the 35,000 survivors from the pocket making their painful way towards the German lines. The breakout had been completed: '. . . a shining example of heroic determination, aggressive spirit and selfless comrade- ship . . .' was how the High Command communiqué described it.

Army Group South concentrated its forces to rebuild its shattered left wing but a new and powerful Soviet blow destroyed it utterly. As the Red Army swept towards the Dniester the German corps, isolated from each other, stood like rocks in the flood. Between First and Fourth

Panzer Armies a gap was torn at Proskurov but before III Corps could seal the breach the whole of First Panzer Army was surrounded in the Kamenz–Podolsk sector. Bitter fighting continued for days as the Soviets strove to destroy the Germans and as the Panzer Corps battled to avoid destruction. A relief force made up of II SS Panzer Corps fought its way from the west and it was with the spearhead units of the SS Corps that the Leibstandarte finally made contact. But of the fresh, well-equipped, élite division which had entered upon the November battles only a battered remnant remained. This cadre of battle-hardened veterans was the nucleus around which a new Leibstandarte was to be built and during the late March days these men began their move westwards to Belgium.

6
Military Operations – 'Festung Europa'

The Normandy Campaign

On 6th June 1944 the Western Allies debarked upon the coast of Normandy. The German High Command, unsure whether these were the real landings or only a feint, had also been uncertain whether to meet the Allied armies on the beach and to drive them back (the Rommel concept) or to destroy them in a grand, formal campaign once they had landed (the Rundstedt theory). In the event they failed to carry out either of their options and with each succeeding week the Allies grew in strength until they were no longer struggling to retain a foothold but were poised ready to burst out of the close confinement of the bridgehead.

The Leibstandarte, which was lying in the area of Bruges in Belgium, was not at first called to the battle. Since spring it had been resting and in April had become part of the High Command strategic reserve and, therefore, under Hitler's direct control. Eleven days after D-Day British Intelligence reported that the 1st SS Panzer Division was moving towards the battle front and very soon thereafter it had begun to concentrate south of Caen, the town which had become the pivot of the Allied line. To loosen the German hold on the town, Montgomery, the British commander, prepared an offensive, codenamed 'Epsom', to force the Odon river and, by reaching the high ground south of the river, to dominate the roads leading to Caen. The assault by VIII and XXX British Corps began on 26th June and despite determined

German resistance achieved certain objectives. At one point during the battle elements of the Leibstandarte were brought in to thicken the line against a threatened breakthrough and on 28th June the first Grenadier companies of the SS Division went in unsupported by their tanks. Allied air attacks had so destroyed cohesion that the Leibstandarte vehicles were strung for many miles along the road from Caen and the mass of the division did not reach the battle area until 9th July. During that day the SS Division, at first in reserve some five or six miles south of Caen, was moved up the line opposite 3rd Canadian Division. Montgomery was 'tidying up' the battlefield prior to opening a new offensive and the Canadians were fighting to seize Hill 112, a strategic feature in the Orne river area. Attack and counter-attack succeeded each other in the cornfields and cultivated Normandy countryside as the SS Grenadiers, with years of combat experience, battled with an Army the greatest number of whose soldiers had seen barely a month's campaigning.

On 18th July Operation 'Goodwood', the second of the British offensives, opened. This was to be an advance by three British armoured divisions to capture the high ground south of Caen, to hold and to weaken Panzer Group West, so as to allow the American Operation 'Cobra' to break out along the Cotentin peninsula.

Operation 'Goodwood' opened with concentrated bombing strikes by the RAF and although the Leibstandarte sectors were outside the bombing areas some elements were attacked and suffered severe losses. At 09.30 hours on the morning of the 18th the Leibstandarte and 21st Panzer Divisions roared off to counter-attack a penetration at Caghy by the Coldstreams of Guards Armoured Division and by units of 11th Armoured Division. For this counter-attack the 1st SS Panzer Division could muster only forty-six armoured fighting vehicles and

some self-propelled guns, but these were formed into a
two-pronged assault. British pressure began to force the
Germans back and it seemed as if a breakthrough into
open country might yet be achieved but the British tanks
ran on to a screen of heavy anti-tank guns manned by III
Flak Corps, the best artillery unit on the Western Front.
The tank thrust faltered and a dynamic counter-attack by
a battle group made up of four Panzer and four infantry
battalions of 1st SS and 21st Panzer Divisions flung back
the spearheads. The British lost more than 200 tanks
while between them the Germans lost 109 tanks – but the
line had held.

On the 19th the British 11th Armoured Division came
on again at Bras and in fierce hand-to-hand fighting wiped
out a Leibstandarte Grenadier battalion. During the 20th,
Canadian II Corps attacked the important Vassières ridge
and smashed through 272nd Infantry Division behind
which the Leibstandarte was in reserve. An *ad hoc* SS
battle group of seventy tanks and a group from 2nd
Panzer Division rushed into an assault and in the heavy
downpour which marked the afternoon of 20th July
crushed the Canadian drive. Operation 'Goodwood' was
called off during the 20th but all through that night and
the following day the Leibstandarte companies battled
hand to hand against men as determined as themselves.
A period of minor activity followed but fighting flared
again on 25th July. At 03.30 hours a British assault struck
down the Caen–Falaise road with 2nd Canadian
Armoured Brigade supporting 3rd Canadian Infantry
Division to capture Tilly-la-Campagne. The 1st SS Panzer
Division, defending the place, reacted swiftly by mounting
an immediate counter-attack which delayed the advance,
and a series of fierce, hard-hitting assaults by the SS
Grenadiers succeeded each other throughout the whole
day and finally drove the Canadians back. Casualties to

the Canadians were unusually high and the Tank Brigade was virtually destroyed as a fighting unit.

During the time that the British had been making their attacks towards Falaise the Americans opened Operation 'Cobra', their own breakout attempt. A gap torn in the line during the fierce fighting of 25th July had been so widened and exploited that by 31st July the German defence in the Cotentin peninsula had been completely smashed and the Americans began to outflank the armies in the south of the peninsula.

Hitler's military solution to this disaster was as simple as it was unreal. Cherbourg was to be regained and Seventh German Army, weakened by weeks of combat, was ordered to split the US First and Third Armies by advancing upon Avranches, to roll them up and to destroy them between Avranches and Mortain, thus sealing the Cotentin front. The spearhead of the attack was to be 2nd Panzer Division reinforced by a Panzer battalion from the Leibstandarte and one from 116th Panzer Division. Once a breach had been made the SS Division, minus the detached battalion and a regiment of Panzer Grenadiers, was to exploit the situation and to capture Avranches. Accordingly, on 3rd August, the Leibstandarte was withdrawn from the British front and ordered to move south-east to the US sector, using best possible speed. This last injunction meant a considerable risk, for the Division hurrying to the attack would be risking the assaults of the Allied Air Forces. In fact the daily wastage rate suffered by units in the field during the move rose to 30 to 40 per cent, this representing an increase of ten to fourteen times above the average. The Leibstandarte was learning the Anglo-American concept of war and a report by a German officer stated '. . . it has had no experience of fighter-bomber attacks on this scale'. So severe were the delays that less than two hours before zero hour the SS

Division was still six miles short of the start-line and zero hour had to be postponed.

One arm of the attack went in at midnight of 6th–7th August against the US troops garrisoning St Albaye Blanche and the second pincer, made up of 2nd Panzer Division and its Leibstandarte component, went in at dawn and overran part of the 117th Division which was defending St Barthélemy. The assault was made in misty conditions and under low cloud which reduced Allied air activity, but by midday this concealment had been dispersed and the Leibstandarte columns were caught strung out on the open road and severely battered. During mid-morning the SS was ordered to revive the bogged-down attack by 2nd Panzer and to capture Juvigny. But severe losses caused by air strikes paralysed the thrust and it ground to a halt. Hitler's grandiose plan had failed, for, due to lack of co-ordination, only three of the six assault columns had moved off on time. The High Command proposed that the offensive be halted but Hitler was still confident that a continuation would '. . . bring about the collapse of the [US] Normandy Front . . .' and gave orders that it be continued. Although the Generals of the High Command did not feel that Hitler's offensive to drive the Allies into the sea had any hope of realization, they accepted that the future role of their armies on the Western Front was a defensive one and they were confident that they could form a line against which the armies of the Western Allies could be held and bled to death.

But British pressure in the north and the American drive in the south were creating a pocket which threatened the German field armies in France with containment and destruction. Hitler's order to reopen the offensive brought the 1st SS and the 2nd Panzer Divisions to a new concentration area on 13th August, ready to begin the offensive anew. The chaos produced in the SS Division by

Allied air strikes resulted in the arrival of the Artillery, then of the Signals Battalion, then the armoured vehicles and finally, on 14th August, the Grenadiers. It was apparent that the new offensive ordered for the 15th August had no hope of success and that, in fact, the German armies were almost completely surrounded. On 16th August the High Command ordered a withdrawal and during the 18th and 19th the Leibstandarte began to move through the line held by II Paratroop Corps. During the few hours of darkness the German columns ground slowly forward, at some points eight vehicles abreast, driving in thick, autumn fog through the heavily wooded countryside towards the Dives river. By the afternoon of the 20th the Leibstandarte and 2nd Panzer Division, concentrated in the Gouffern forest, had broken out in the St Lambert–Chambois area and the SS Division was moved for refitting behind the Seine river.

The Battle of Normandy was over for 1st SS Panzer Division and it had suffered almost total destruction. On 13th August its total armoured strength had been less than thirty serviceable vehicles: fourteen Mark IV, seven Mark V and eight self-propelled guns. The breakout had occasioned it further losses and only remnants of the division which had left Flanders in late June survived to reach the rehabilitation area in late August.

Normandy had cost the Germans 160,000 men and the Allies 180,000 men. But Allied strength was certain to increase as follow-up divisions arrived. To cover their losses the German Army in the West received only 30,000 replacements. A German victory in the West was an unrealizable ambition. A military stalemate along a line of fortifications was the best it could hope for with the most likely fate being the destruction of the Army west of the Rhine.

The Ardennes Offensive: The Battle of the Bulge

By the end of 1944 the tides in the fortunes of war were flowing strongly against Germany. On the land fronts and in the air her enemies were preparing blows which would destroy her. Germany was everywhere on the defensive but in the mind of Adolf Hitler there was a conviction that a bold counter-stroke in the West would capture Antwerp, split the Anglo-American forces and lead to another, greater Dunkirk.

The plan for such a counter-stroke, drawn up at Hitler's direction, proposed an attack from the Ardennes, the classic invasion route from Germany to the West and the area from which the successful 1940 campaign had been launched. The date, however, could not be immediately established, for this was dependent upon how long it took to assemble the required numbers of men, tanks, aeroplanes and supplies. In the event 16th December was reluctantly accepted by Hitler.

The intention was that three armies, Sixth SS Panzer, Fifth Panzer and Seventh Panzer, would attack along a seventy-mile front. The Sixth SS Panzer was virtually an SS Army and was given the task of forming the main assault unit. Its I SS Panzer Corps would form a wave which would reach and cross the Maas and then, leapfrogging over the bridgeheads which had been created, the II SS Panzer Corps would carry the assault forward to Antwerp. The Anglo-Canadian forces north of the line Antwerp–Liège–Ardennes would then be rolled up.

The strictest security was observed. So well kept was the secret of the operation that von Rundstedt, the man whom Hitler had chosen to be its Supreme Commander, was not told of the plan until less than seven weeks before D-Day. The commanders of units essential to the execution of the plan, the parachute troops and Skorzeny's group of American-speaking Germans who were to capture bridges and to spread confusion in the American rear areas, had barely enough time to select their men; training them adequately was out of the question. Regimental commanders were told of their part in the attack only on the day preceding the assault. Hitler's personal control of the planning was so tight that he even dictated the axes of advance of some units, particularly that of the 1st SS Panzer Division's Combat Group, upon whom the success or failure of the operation can be said to have depended. The Combat Group, led by Jochen Peiper, is the unit with which this account of the Leibstandarte's part in the Ardennes offensive is chiefly concerned, for the Battle of the Bulge is very much the story of Kampfgruppe Peiper.

Peiper was the personification of the perfect SS man: handsome, young, dedicated and loyal. Bold and aggressive in action, he was a skilled soldier who spared neither himself nor his men and certainly never the enemy, but who would do his uttermost to prevent the waste of his men's lives. His professional ability had given him command of the most important unit in the Sixth SS Army – probably the most important unit in the whole battle line – and his superiors believed that the ruthlessness which he had shown in Russia would force the victory to be his in this the decisive battle in the West.

His Kampfgruppe, with a strength of about 5,000 men, was made up of 1st Panzer Battalion of 2nd SS Panzer Grenadier Regiment, SS Reconnaissance Battalion, artillery, anti-aircraft guns, Pioneers, Engineers and Services. Most of his men were old campaigners, despite their youth; hard, tough men who would follow Peiper wherever he led. His task was to move this force with all possible speed, ignoring threats to his flanks, across a region totally unsuitable for armoured vehicles. His route was laid down by Hitler and no deviation from it was allowed. From Losheim he was to advance westwards through Honsfeld and via Schoppen to Baugnez. The direction would change at that point southwards towards Ligneuville and then westwards again to Stavelot on the Amblève river, arriving, finally, at Trois Ponts. Up to that point the advance would have been a difficult one because of the poor roads and few bridges, but once through Trois Ponts the going would be easier. At Werbemont there would be a halt to concentrate the column and then there would be the final dash for Huy on the Maas. Guarding Peiper's left flank during the early part of the advance would be six mechanized squadrons of the Reconnaissance Battalion. This group would rejoin the Command after crossing the Bastogne–Liège road.

The success of the plan depended upon the Kampfgruppe being able to break out of the Amblève river valley and this it could only do if the few bridges capable of bearing the weight of heavy tanks were captured intact. Hitler's attention to detail had determined the precise routes of advance but the Führer had failed to ensure adequate and regular supplies of fuel to the armoured columns. The commanders were expected to capture from American dumps the petrol sufficient for their needs.

With hindsight it is easy to see that the Americans only needed to deny petrol to the Panzers, to destroy the river bridges and to contain the German thrust by local attacks until they had built up sufficient strength to launch their decisive counter-blows. This is what they did to the Kampfgruppe Peiper and the Battle of the Bulge on that sector of the front can be summarized in the phrase: a fight for fuel and a battle for bridges.

To the Germans speed was the most essential factor both in the immediate and in the long term. Speed in the short term would be required to capture the bridges, and in the long term it was necessary to make an advance so rapid that Antwerp could be reached before the Allies could react effectively. The speed at which the spearheading Sixty SS Panzer Army could advance was conditional upon the number, type and condition of the roads which had been allotted to it. In the event only five routes forward were allowed to Dietrich's forces; the whole bulk of his Army would have to traverse difficult terrain on a road network insufficient in number and poor in quality.

But the vital role which Sixth SS Panzer Army was to play was underlined by other advantages that were given it. With nine divisions, four of them SS Panzer divisions, it was the most powerful army. It held the narrowest front – Rötgen to Losheim – and it had the shortest distance to travel to reach the final objective. The main disadvantage was the fact that it faced difficult country: a succession of wooded ridges, deep river valleys and poor roads. Dietrich calculated that despite this disadvantage he could still be able to establish bridgeheads across the Maas by the fourth day of the offensive.

Priess, Commander of I SS Panzer Corps, forming the left flank of Sixth Panzer Army, decided to make his breakthrough point in the lightly held, seven-mile-wide Losheim Gap, an area of rolling country offering better chances of exploitation and movement than other sectors. His plan was to breach the American line using a Parachute and a Volksgrenadier Division. This latter would have only hours to accomplish its mission and then through the gap which had been torn would pour Kampfgruppe Peiper, spearheading the advance of the Leibstandarte Division and of Sixth SS Panzer Army racing for the Maas only seventy-odd miles away.

The 1st SS Panzer Division was the strongest fighting unit in Sixth SS Panzer Army. During the weeks of its period out of the line it had been brought up to strength and equipped with the most modern tanks. Forty-two

King Tigers, formed into No. 501 SS Panzer Battalion, were on establishment, in addition to the standard Mark IV, Mark V Panther and Mark VI Tiger tanks. Losses in men had been made good with first-class replacements and the soldiers of the division were eager for action, not least to avenge the civilian population of Düren, in the Rhineland, whose bodies they had had to clear following a particularly heavy Allied air raid on that city.

Because of the poor road system in the divisional sector, the Leibstandarte could not be committed to the fight as a whole. The advance would be undertaken as a group of four columns. The first of these was Peiper's Kampfgruppe on the most northerly of the divisional axes. On the left flank of Peiper's group would be six of the Reconnaissance Battalion's squadrons serving as a link between the Kampfgruppe and the mass of the division driving on the southern route. The two columns of this latter group would contain armoured infantry and heavy weapons. The 501 SS Panzer Battalion would be fitted into the battle as and when the need arose.

During the first two weeks of December a vast movement of men and materials was carried out all over western Germany. To transport just the men and machines of the Leibstandarte Division to its concentration area required more than 200 trains; and there were four Panzer Divisions in the Sixth SS Army assault. By 12th December the troops of all three armies were in position twelve miles behind the front line and, during the following day, the infantry elements were brought closer to the fighting zone. The take-over from units holding forward positions was so secret that preliminary reconnaissance by officers of incoming formations was forbidden, nor were tactical signs for those units erected lest they betrayed the presence of new troops. By nightfall on 13th December, the artillery, driving on muffled wheels, had been brought up, but the armour, some 900 vehicles in all, was still in position in the holding area, twelve miles behind the line.

Two days later a total of twenty-two German divisions, numbering perhaps a quarter of a million men, was facing four and a half American divisions. Everything was ready for the assault. The several Orders of the Day from the Supreme Commander down to division level stressed the importance of the imminent offensive; everyone now waited for zero hour. But not quite everyone, for shortly before 05.30 hours German patrols infiltrated the forward US positions killing sentries and cutting wires. The icy cold had reduced activity on the American side and the howling, gale-force wind drowned the clatter of the German tank columns as they rolled westwards. Operation 'Autumn Fog' was about to begin. On D-Day, Saturday 16th December, at about 04.00 hours on a dark and bitter winter morning, Peiper's group of tanks began to roll towards the front. Ahead of the column the dark December sky was suddenly split with light as the guns of the artillery opened fire in a forty-five-minute-long drum-fire upon the forward American positions. As suddenly as it had begun the barrage ceased, only to begin again at 08.00 hours on the rear areas. Behind the initial barrage stormed the Assault divisions of 1st SS Panzer Corps. Under pressure the American line bent but did not rupture and Dietrich was compelled to put 12th SS Panzer Division prematurely into action to smash a way through the US front. Not only had the Assault divisions been unable to break the American front but certain villages of local strategic importance had not been taken. The elaborate time-table was already out of schedule.

On the routes leading to the front there was confusion as the columns of tanks, artillery and infantry struggled forward on the blocked roads and Peiper waited impatiently for the way to clear and to let him through. A visit to the Headquarters of 12th Volksgrenadier Division proved unproductive and, soon after 15.00 hours, he ordered his column to advance towards Losheim. But a direct drive on that place was not possible as both Losheimgraben and Hunningen were still in the hands of the Americans. During the short six-mile move Peiper exhibited that ruthlessness in pursuit of an objective for which he was famous throughout the Waffen SS. Finding the road blocked by slow-moving horse-artillery columns of the Volksgrenadier Division he ordered his driver to roll over anything and everything in his way. Shortly after 19.30 hours he was in Losheim where he received an order from Corps to turn west to Lanzerath and to get the 3rd Parachute Division's attack moving again. Krewinckel, which had been taken by the main body of the Leibstandarte, should have helped forward the paratroop advance but this was not the case. The SS had to spur the attack. Peiper swung his column westwards and found the Lanzerath road blocked with anti-tank mines. Without hesitation he ordered the column to advance and lost five vehicles before the mined area had been crossed. The armoured column then drove along primitive paths in the dense pine forests to avoid the heavy artillery fire which the Americans were laying on all the roads to Stavelot.

At about midnight, in the artificial moonlight of reflected searchlight beams, Jochen Peiper and the commander of 9th Parachute Regiment met and were soon involved in a fierce argument on the future employment of the paratroops by the SS commander. Peiper commandeered a whole battalion and mounted them on the tanks of his waiting column. The advance was ordered and with the heavy reconnaissance vehicles of SS Hauptsturmführer Preuss's No. 10 Company leading the way, the Kampfgruppe roared towards the final

objective. By 01.00 hours on Sunday 17th December the
SS column was approaching Honsfeld. Peiper found that
the Buchholz–Honsfeld road was choked with American
vehicles and men retreating westwards. Calmly he waited
until there was a break in the columns and into this gap
inserted his Kampfgruppe, headed by two captured
Sherman tanks. Thus concealed he entered and captured
the little town of Honsfeld as well as a considerable
amount of booty. The route forward for 1st SS Panzer
Division was now clear.

The first day had seen crises for both sides. The
breakthrough and the dissolution of the American front
which the Germans had anticipated had just not happened. The vital element of surprise had been lost and
many staff officers were in favour of breaking off the
whole offensive, for the elaborate time-table was now
unworkable. On the American side the crisis was one of
uncertainty and the reports of German armoured spearheads not only threatened the Headquarters of 99th
Division but also the ordnance and fuel depots of V
Corps, containing millions of gallons of petrol, and for
the defence of which no troops were available. Even at
Army level the anxiety about the German thrusts manifested itself in the hurried evacuation, some days later, of
the Headquarters from Spa to Liège.

The route as laid out by Hitler directed that the advance
continue via Schoppen but that road was a mass of slush
and mud. To the north lay a road with a paved surface
and, more important still, with an American dump not
too far away at Bullinghen. Both lay on the 12th SS
Panzer Division's axis of advance. In defiance of a direct
order Peiper did not hesitate and sent the armoured
vehicles of Preuss's 10th Company on a reconnaissance.
Preuss found the dump and captured it together with
twelve airworthy planes which were on the nearby airfield.
Soon the vehicles of Peiper's Kampfgruppe were being

filled with the unwilling assistance of US soldiers who had been captured. These operations did not go without interference from dug-in American tanks whose fire destroyed two Mark IV vehicles and from US artillery which bombarded him. By midday the column was back on its own route and, south of Morscheck, Peiper divided his column to carry out a pincer attack upon Ligneuville, a small town some miles to the west. The group which he led thrust along the correct route while the second detachment of tanks and Grenadiers advanced on his right flank along minor tracks and roads. Peiper's column met with no difficulty but the northern group encountered, opened fire upon and captured a small artillery column of 7th US Armored Division which was driving southwards towards the Baugnez crossroads. It was in a field near this tiny hamlet of six houses that the American prisoners of this northern column were massacred. Both German columns arrived in Ligneuville in time to eat the lunch which had been prepared for the US garrison. The Kampfgruppe was joined by Mohnke, the Divisional Commander, who had come forward to see how the attack was progressing.

Outside the town tanks of 9th Armored Division, the first mobile American armoured fighting vehicles that the Kampfgruppe had met during its advance, opened fire and in a short fight destroyed two personnel carriers and a Panther for the loss of two Shermans and a tank destroyer. Late in the afternoon the advance was resumed towards Stavelot where Peiper intended to cross the Amblève river, for the bridge there was capable of bearing the weight of the Tiger tanks. At last light the lead vehicles edged round a huge rock and below him Peiper could see the little town and the unblown bridge. In the fading vision masses of American vehicles could be seen moving through the town. An immediate attack was ordered to capture the bridge and the Tiger tanks of No.

6 Company manoeuvred themselves round the corner of the road and headed downhill. The lead tank hit an American mine and lost its track. Scraping together his only available infantry – sixty Grenadiers – Peiper launched them into the assault. They were beaten back by rifle and machine-gun fire, supported by artillery and anti-tank guns. It seemed that there was no way forward. The strung-out columns of Peiper's group closed up on the advanced guard and the exhausted men bedded down for the night only forty-two miles from the Maas. Little did the SS commander realize how few were the Americans opposing him, nor could he appreciate that the failure to press home the attack gave the US forces in the area a breathing space in which to build up their defences. Peiper's decision was, perhaps, influenced by the exhaustion of his men and the mass of American vehicles which he had observed in the streets of Stavelot.

During the evening Divisional Headquarters came forward to Manderfeld and in the late evening of 17th December a conference was held which decided that Skorzeny's troops would fight as ordinary infantry.

On the US side the news of the Malmédy massacre had spread rapidly and produced the effect in 328th Infantry Regiment of a written order that no SS man would be taken prisoner but would be shot on sight.

In the early hours of 18th December, elements of the SS Panzer Grenadier Regiment travelling with the main divisional group seized Recht, but the mass of the Leibstandarte Division was still strung out in the monster traffic jams which still clogged the German rear areas. A naval officer of Skorzeny's Command brought this information to the Kampfgruppe and added that no reinforcement could, therefore, be expected. Peiper decided to press on without support and sent out patrols which were in contact with the Americans as early as 05.00 hours on a foggy, cold day. Some hours later German infantry and tanks, advancing behind a short, fierce barrage, assaulted the Stavelot bridge. Two Panthers and a Grenadier company stormed downhill at top speed and although the first Panther was hit the momentum carried it through the flimsy barricade while the second tank crossed the stone bridge, leading a column of machines which had soon captured the southern half of the town. Even while the fighting was in progress Peiper detached a squadron of tanks to capture Trois Ponts, the most important of the river crossings in the Amblève valley.

Nineteen tanks of the Kampfgruppe advanced guard roared down upon Trois Ponts, but two of these vital bridges, one over the Amblève and one over the Salm river, were blown as the Panzers reached them, forcing Peiper to look for a by-pass route. His map showed that to the north on a poor road passing through La Gleize he would find an exit to the west. By midday the head of his column had reached the mountain village of La Gleize and had halted among the small stone houses of the single street. A reconnaissance detachment went out and captured a bridge at nearby Cheneux and the column then passed over this and headed for Habiemont.

American reaction to the movement of Peiper's Kampfgruppe was now taking the form of local, offensive operations. During the course of one small counter-attack launched by a battalion of 117th Infantry Regiment with the object of capturing Stavelot, a line of ten German tanks was located. A lucky bazooka hit not only destroyed one of the vehicles but its bulk effectively blocked the narrow, main street, adding to the congestion which had been worsened by the arrival of part of the Reconnaissance Battalion.

To the north of the German salient was positioned part of 30th Infantry Division, moving in from the west and from the south-west. They linked and a ring, weak but becoming stronger, was being cast around the Kampfgruppe on the ground. In the skies, too, there was action. Soon after midday aeroplanes of 9th Tactical Air Command began the first of a series of attacks upon the rear of the strung-out column of German vehicles on the Stavelot–Lodomez road and between 14.00 hours and the onset of dusk the Thunderbolt fighter-bombers swept down upon the head of the column as it crossed the Amblève river near Cheneux and during its subsequent advance along the line of the woods near Rahier. Three tanks and seven other vehicles were destroyed during these sorties. Under constant and heavy assault Peiper could only order his unit to disperse and the advance was not resumed until after dark. Both sides now realized that unless the Kampfgruppe could break out from the Amblève valley it could advance no further westwards. One possible escape route was by a bridge across the Liènne. The advance was continued towards this escape route but the bridge was blown in the faces of the leading tank crews. With characteristic decisiveness Peiper ordered a return to La Gleize with the intention of taking the column back to Stoumont and then north-west to Awayville. This was a long and almost impossible route but was one by which he might still reach Liège. In attempting this route Peiper was being forced to strike in a northerly direction, precisely that direction which Kraemer, the Chief of Staff, did not wish him to go, for in that direction lay huge, enemy forces of unknown but immense power. One advanced detachment, accompanied by half tracks and assault guns, searching for a second escape route found a bridge and prepared to move on Werbemont but US troops armed with bazookas ambushed the column and drove it back.

Peiper's Kampfgruppe then bivouacked on what was to

be, on the morrow, the battlefield of Stoumont. A measure of the confidence which the SS men still possessed is
shown in the report of a US patrol from 3rd Battalion.
119th Infantry which found a laager of about thirty enemy
vehicles with the crews singing round a blazing campfire.
This confidence was in part due to ignorance. For days
the Kampfgruppe had been out of wireless contact with
Headquarters and was, therefore, unaware of what was
happening on other sectors, particularly of American
reactions and counter-moves. Neither Peiper nor his men
could be aware that failures at High Command level in
co-ordinating the offensive were slowing it down. St Vith,
a vital road centre through which a steady flow of supplies
and reinforcements might have been expected to flow to
the Kampfgruppe, had remained uncaptured. So long as
it remained in American hands the Peiper group was
being strangled. St Vith lay on the boundary of Fifth and
Sixth SS Panzer Armies. The Fifth had wanted to take the
place but Dietrich had his eyes fixed firmly on the far
objective and was only interested in moving westwards to
Antwerp. Manteuffel's Fifth Army was compelled to keep
pace with Dietrich and St Vith remained a thorn in the
German side until its capture.

American counter-moves were gaining ground but only
slowly, for the fighting everywhere was bitter. On the
southern flank a part of 2nd SS Panzer Grenadier Regiment struck south-west from Recht, crossed the Recht
river and headed for the important road and railway
junction of Poteau. The possession of that place was vital
for American troop movements and spirited attacks were
launched by 48th Armored Infantry Battalion of 7th
Armored Division. As the American tanks came near
Poteau they were engaged by artillery and machine-guns
of the Leibstandarte Grenadiers but pressed their assault
with vigour until they held part of the village. Tank

destroyers, assault guns and tanks hunted each other cautiously among the few houses but the American pressure was too great. The men of the SS cannot have been said to have withdrawn from the village; they fought to the last and died where they fought.

On the southern flank, too, the mass of 2nd Panzer Grenadier Regiment spent the day fighting its way towards Wanne, with the intention of linking up with Peiper at Trois Ponts.

At daybreak on 19th December, Peiper opened the battle which he was determined would carry him out of the Amblève river valley. Around Stoumont the country was more open than that in which he had been fighting for the past days and much of it was level, cultivated fields. He formed his Kampfgruppe into two massive columns to make a classic pincer movement. For this attack he had gathered nearly the whole of his Command, including the King Tiger Battalion (which had joined him at Stavelot), a battery of 105mm self-propelled guns and a company of parachutists. This impressive array of armour advanced through the thick mist undeterred by the weak American defensive fire. Ten tanks from US 743rd Battalion came up to stiffen the defence but the German tactic of rushing two tanks forward at top speed drove the Americans back, though not without loss to the Panzers, for six of them were immobilized or destroyed during the course of the fighting. But by midday Stoumont, except for the railway station, was in German hands. The move towards Targon, at which place the column would turn south-west to capture Chevron and thereby escape from the Amblève valley, had to be delayed until Stoumont station was captured, for the high ground around the station dominated the area through which Peiper's tanks must pass to reach Targon. The fighting for the station was long and confused but as

minute succeeded minute without a decisive victory the
realization grew in Peiper's mind that he was running out
of fuel and could not afford to fight a protracted battle.
He now had insufficient petrol to strike for Targon. He
had no alternative. Reluctantly, he accepted the inevitable and ordered a withdrawal to Stoumont and La
Gleize.

The head of the Kampfgruppe was concentrated in
strength around Stoumont, La Gleize and Cheneux while
the tail was fighting to hold Stavelot and thereby keep
open a route to the rear. Then came the news that
American troops had captured Stavelot and had blown
the bridge. The 3rd German Parachute Division should
have defended the place but their advance had been
delayed by the clogged roads in the German rear areas.
Peiper's reaction was immediate and he ordered tanks
and infantry into the assault to drive out the 1st Battalion
of 117th Infantry, which was now holding the town.

Co-ordinated with the counter-attack of the 2nd SS
Panzer Grenadier Regiment and six Tiger tanks was an
advance by two companies of the Reconnaissance Battalion but American artillery smashed back these with
heavy loss. Mohnke, the divisional commander, formed
ad hoc battle groups from detachments which he inter-
cepted on the road near Petit Spai and set them in motion
along the southern road. By 13.00 hours this relieving
column had captured Wanne and had taken up a position
near Petit Spai bridge by the late afternoon. Throughout
the winter afternoon and evening the fighting continued
and the point which the relief column held at midnight
marked the farthest western point which the Leibstandarte was to reach. Thereafter it would be forced back,
eventually to be put into the line near St Vith.

The Sixth SS Panzer Army had failed in its attempt to
broaden the extent of the breakthrough area sufficient for

the second wave to sweep forward and, indeed, the fastest advances were being made by Fifth Panzer Army. Appreciating this fact the German High Command took the task of exploitation from Dietrich's SS and gave it to Fifth Army. In Sixth SS Army sector the main effort was now no longer being made by Peiper and it was Dietrich's intention to push north-west in the Salm river sector.

Having tried to take Stavelot by armoured assault and failed the Germans tried a new approach and sent the Panzer Grenadiers wading across the icy cold Amblève during the early morning hours of 20th December. The badly co-ordinated attacks failed as the attackers died under the barrage of fire which was poured down upon them. Undeterred by this failure the SS tried again and yet again, struggling slowly through the fast-running, thigh-high water. Silhouetted against the light of burning houses and flares, the American riflemen could not miss such targets and drove back the slow-moving Grenadiers to their own side of the river. But only to re-form and, showing incredible courage, to storm forward once again and this time with such *élan* that some of them actually reached the American-held shore and tried to establish a bridgehead. These few were killed where they fought.

During 20th December, the Americans, having stabilized the northern flank, set out to destroy the Kampfgruppe in the Stoumont–La Gleize sector.

Through the thick fog which covered the battlefield units of 30th Division, with the support of armoured fighting vehicles from 740th Tank Battalion, the Americans moved down during the late afternoon in a three-column attack upon Peiper's Kampfgruppe. Although immobilized from lack of petrol the SS units were by no means impotent and they mauled the attackers severely. One US column lost six tanks, the second lost two and the infantry assault was beaten into the ground. The inevitable German counter-attack smashed against those troops who had managed to enter the little town of Stoumont. Savage, hand-to-hand fighting took place in and around the sanatorium of St Edward which dominated the place. German tanks rumbling forward in support of the Grenadiers fired their heavy guns through the windows of the hospital and drove out many of the Americans, but then the US troops came in with their counter-attack and forced the SS to withdraw.

At Cheneux, on the southern sector of the German salient, the 1st Battalion of 82nd Airborne Division's 504th Regiment mounted four waves of attacks against the Panzer Grenadiers. Three successive waves of Airborne soldiers stormed across the 400 yards of open ground laced with barbed wire, but in the waist-high fire of the light Flak guns their attacks collapsed. The Germans were wreaking revenge for the losses which the Americans had caused them during their own assaults across the Amblève. A fourth attack succeeded in reducing the size of the bridgehead and the US soldiers stalked the Flak guns, which had caused them such casualties, with grenade and knife. No quarter was asked or given.

Five days of the offensive had run their course and Peiper had still not cleared the Amblève river valley. At Headquarters the question was now no longer whether the Maas would be crossed but how quickly it would be possible to extricate the Kampfgruppe from the pocket in which it was surrounded. On the American side there was the realization that the US forces now had the measure of the enemy and plans were laid to contain him in an even closer pocket. But the General Officer commanding 30th Division was concerned lest the Leibstandarte carry out a successful attack north of Trois Ponts and break the ring which his division and 82nd Airborne had cast. As a matter of the utmost priority Peiper's group in the La Gleize–Stoumont sector had to be destroyed.

At a midday conference in the Château Froid Couer, Peiper reviewed the situation. He told his officers that Sixth SS Army was to begin an attack on Malmédy which would open the road forward towards Antwerp and provide the Kampfgruppe with an escape route. Divisional Headquarters had informed him that the bulk of the Leibstandarte would make a breakthrough attempt from the south but he himself had no illusions. The military situation in the pocket was deteriorating and he had decided to withdraw from Stoumont to La Gleize retaining the Cheneux bridgehead. Thus there would still be a base from which to break out and exploit when the bulk of the Division relieved him at the anticipated meeting point of Trois Ponts.

The German relief attempts began with a heavy bombardment which swamped the American batteries. 1st SS Panzer Grenadier Regiment in the south struck 2nd Battalion of the Airborne Regiment and it seemed as if the Leibstandarte might break through and yet force the line of the Amblève. But the timely arrival of US reinforcements turned the scale and the small bridgehead which the Grenadiers had managed to establish was the scene of bitter fighting between the Panzer Grenadiers and the 2nd Battalion of the Airborne Infantry. The sodden ground halted the deployment of the German armour and the battle was that of knots of infantry fighting in swirling mist around the stranded, armoured vehicles. Hand-to-hand combat was the norm in this struggle for the bridgehead and at last it was reduced and destroyed. There were no unwounded German survivors; true to their established tradition they had fought to the last man.

The Sixth SS Panzer Army had meanwhile captured St Vith but as a counter-balance the Cheneux bridgehead

had been taken out by the Airborne. The greatest number
of the SS made good their withdrawal leaving behind a
determined rearguard which fought with customary
devotion to duty. The cost to the Americans in this final,
fourth assault was no less than 225 dead and wounded.

At 16.00 hours on 21st December the Kampfgruppe
Headquarters together with the walking wounded withdrew to the two streets of houses which formed the hamlet
of La Gleize. The German forces in Stoumont were still
denying possession of the sanatorium to the Americans
and repeated their tactic of firing tank guns through the
windows of the hospital.

Snow began to fall during the early hours of 22nd
December and the temperature dropped quickly, bringing
even more misery to the fighting troops of both sides.
Americans probing into La Gleize had been driven off
with heavy loss. Although Peiper was out of radio contact
with the Division, the Commander, Mohnke, was aware
of the difficulties of his subordinate and ordered an air
drop. At 14.00 hours three Luftwaffe machines dropped
ammunition and fuel, but the quantities were insufficient
for less than 10 per cent of the drop landed within the
target area.

American long-range guns then began to bombard La
Gleize, setting alight some of the thirty houses. Peiper,
suffering casualties from a bombardment to which he
could make no reply, requested permission to break out.
His force was divided; one part was under pressure from
504th Regiment's 3rd Battalion holding the ground
between Cheneux and the Amblève river. At La Gleize
troops of 30th Division were attacking and along the
valley road south of Stoumont patrols were probing east
of La Gleize. Other units of 30th Division attacked the
pockets of Germans who had succeeded in crossing the
Amblève river near Stavelot with the intent of linking up

with Peiper. Along the Salm river the Leibstandarte engineers were trying to build bridges to ferry the bulk of the Division across the river, but their efforts were brought to naught by the American 505th Infantry.

Saturday, 23rd December, dawned clear and bright. During the night a second air drop had been carried out but this had had as little success as that of the previous day. In the early afternoon a US infantry attack, put in with the intention of capturing La Gleize, was destroyed by Tiger tanks but the Americans gained so much ground that there was house-to-house fighting in the village and in the late afternoon the American artillery ceased firing for fear of hitting its own troops.

Peiper was now determined to break out and reach his own lines. His Kampfgruppe could no longer serve any useful purpose in its present position; it was short of men, ammunition and, most important, fuel. At 17.00 hours Divisional Headquarters gave the formal permission, adding the proviso that the wounded and the vehicles must accompany the breakout. It was evident that some officers at Command level were unable to appreciate the seriousness of Peiper's position.

To the south the Leibstandarte bridgehead on the north bank of the Amblève was under pressure near Stavelot and, later the same evening, much of the Reconnaissance Company was captured on the Trois Ponts road.

Between 02.00 hours and 03.00 hours on the morning of Christmas Eve, 800 men, the remnants of Kampfgruppe Peiper, marched quietly southwards towards the Amblève river. Behind them in the broken village of La Gleize they had left the wounded and the vehicles. Peiper had used his own Iron Cross to decorate Junker, No. 6 Company Commander in the Panzer Regiment, who had been severely wounded in the fighting. A small rearguard had the task of holding off the US forces until the main body had escaped and until the vehicles had been destroyed.

At 05.00 hours the sky was lit by flames as the mass of armour and vehicles concentrated in La Gleize was set alight. Despite the best efforts of the rearguard twenty-eight tanks, seventy half-tracks and twenty-five guns were captured intact by the US forces next day, but more than thirty tanks and a hundred half-tracks were destroyed by fire. Peiper's total losses came to ninety-two tanks, twenty-three artillery pieces (tractor drawn), seven self-propelled guns, twenty-five armoured rocket projectors, ninety-five half-tracks, sixty-seven trucks and other vehicles and over 2,000 men.

The La Gleize rearguard of fifty men fought to the death. In the woods north of the village other Grenadiers, part of the force which had tried to break through to Peiper, were attacked by infantry of the American 117th and 120th Regiments. Fierce and bitter fighting took place in the dense and snowy woods until the last of these isolated groups of SS men were destroyed.

The Leibstandarte bridgehead on the high ground at Stavelot was assaulted by infantry and tanks of 3rd Armored Division acting in concert with Thunderbolt aircraft of the US Air Force. Under this heavy pressure the 1st SS Panzer Division's columns withdrew across the river.

Peiper's group, meanwhile, had moved via the La Gleize railway station over the Amblève and across the lines of the 505th Regiment of 82nd Airborne Division. By a strange coincidence both the Germans and the Americans were pulling back. When their paths crossed, and they did on a few occasions during that crystal clear, bitterly cold night, the SS went in to kill silently and the small group made its way to the Salm river. This final obstacle they swam or forded and before dawn had linked up with the bulk of 1st SS Panzer Corps, in whose lines they were given a reception fit for heroes.

On St Stephen's Day, 26th December, the remnants of Kampfgruppe Peiper were moved to St Vith for rehabilitation. On that day the only Germans left on the north bank of the Amblève were the prisoners, the wounded or the dead.

During that day, Field-Marshal Model ordered the Leibstandarte Division, now an armoured division without tanks, to move south. Mohnke gathered tanks from repair shops and by 29th December most of his men were located in the area south of Bastogne. This march across the German lines of communication caused serious congestion in the rear areas to which the American air raids brought further confusion and the Leibstandarte had no more than fifty-five tanks gathered in the divisional sector when it was ordered to mount an attack on 30th December.

The original plan was for the 1st SS Panzer to co-operate with 167th Volksgrenadier Division, a regiment of paratroops and a regiment from the Panzer Lehr Division and to drive through the American lines to cut the Assenois–Hompre road.

During the night of 29th December two columns of tanks from the Leibstandarte Division moved down upon 137th Infantry Regiment holding positions at Villers-la-Bonne Eau and Lutrebois. Before dawn the two Panzer columns moved down on the US-held villages and the Panzer Grenadiers slipped through the dark night and infiltrated the lines of one of the battalions of the 137th Regiment in Lutrebois. American artillery opened up and stopped the tank columns east of the village but an encircling attack to the north succeeded and the Grenadiers advanced down the western road until their advance was checked, in its turn, by heavy fire from US machine-guns. A second column of seven Panzers was spotted from the air moving north of Lutrebois. Four of these were destroyed by US armoured fighting vehicles, two fell victim to the artillery and the survivor ran on to a mine.

Confused and fierce fighting marked most of the morning of the 30th December. Grenadiers from 2nd Regiment, hidden by the thick fog which covered the battlefield, advanced through the thick woods but were caught in the open by armoured infantry and driven back to the shelter of the trees. Just before midday the main body of the Leibstandarte Division moved down the Lutremange–Lutrebois road. The twenty-five tanks of the column were brought under air attack in the middle of the afternoon and seven of them were destroyed. Thirteen tanks moved off the road and into the dense woods south of Lutrebois where they were ambushed. The German column, accompanied by Panzer Grenadiers, ran head first on to a group from 35th Tank Battalion in a hull-down position and were destroyed. The assault guns and the half-tracked infantry vehicles were disabled by a tank destroyer unit.

Although the villages of Lutrebois and Villers-la-Bonne Eau were both taken by the German assault the breakout attempt had failed. The Americans claimed that during this day's battle they destroyed or immobilized more than fifty-five Leibstandarte fighting vehicles but this would mean more SS tanks destroyed than went into action. It is obvious that some German tanks were claimed as victims by two units.

On 1st January 1945, the 1st SS Panzer Division was relieved in the Marvie–Lutremange sector by 167th Volksgrenadier Division and left the Ardennes area for refitting in the Bonn district of the Rhineland.

For the Leibstandarte the Battle of the Bulge was over

and the losses on the German and American sides had been enormous. Nearly 100,000 Germans had been killed, wounded or captured and the Americans had lost 76,000. This battle was unique in the sense that it was the only time in the Western campaign from 6th June 1944 that the Germans had held the overall initiative. The result of the battle showed clearly that the military defeat of Germany was inevitable; it was no longer an expectation but a certainty. The Germans might delay the end but the end was certain.

The Final Campaign: Hungary and Austria

In January 1945 the war which had now lasted sixty-five months was nearing its end. In the west and from the south Anglo-American armies were nearing the heartland of the Reich while in the east a tidal wave of Russian armies was sweeping into Prussia and Silesia with Berlin as the prize upon which the Red commanders had fixed their eyes. The Leibstandarte expected that it would be sent to defend endangered Berlin but Hitler had another and, to his mind, far more important priority. Budapest, the capital city of Hungary, had fallen after a long siege and the Leibstandarte together with the rest of Sixth SS Panzer Army was not only to recapture Budapest from the Soviets but was to go on and capture the Hungarian oil wells which Hitler had concluded were essential to the further prosecution of the war. The attack, to be known as Operation 'Spring Awakening', would be unexpected by the Russians for it would go in from the south-west of Budapest, and with the combined assets of surprise and strength there was reason to hope that the whole of the Russian south wing would be rolled up. When 'Sepp' Dietrich met Hitler for the last time, in mid-January, he was given the first objectives of his Army: to reach

Budapest and to establish bridgeheads on the eastern
bank of the Danube.

The divisions of Sixth SS Panzer Army, part of the
massive force which was mustered for the operation, left
the Rhineland in 290 trains and soon the IV SS Corps was
concentrated north of Komorn. If the absence of the SS
Panzer Army from the Intelligence maps baffled and
worried the Western and Eastern allies, for neither was
aware of the exact location of this élite force, then its
presence brought promise to the worn-out veterans of
Army Group South. With new hope rising in their hearts
they saw the long columns of new tanks and guns, the
keen, well-uniformed and splendidly equipped men. Not
privy to Hitler's sense of priorities the front-line soldiers
reasoned that if Germany could still produce such masses
of men and equipment for an unimportant front like
Hungary then things could not be all that bad back home.

Army Group South lay in a great arc west of the
Danube with its boundaries extending from the Drau to
the western edge of Lake Balaton. Then the line swung
westwards to the Vertes mountains and then to a bridgehead which the Russians had established on the northern
bank of the Danube at Gran. The SS Panzer Army, once
more on the strength of the Army Group, took part in a
lightning assault on 17th February when Eighth Army,
with I SS Panzer Corps temporarily under command,
destroyed the Gran bridgehead. The Leibstandarte fought
with its customary efficiency and one of the Knight's
Crosses awarded for this action went to a Panther tank
commander whose victories during one day's fighting
amounted to eleven tanks of the Josef Stalin pattern. The
fighting lasted until 24th February and the cost both to
the Russians and to the SS was high with losses in tanks
to the Panzer Corps being exceptionally severe. The
Corps strength was forty-two tanks surviving from the

full-strength regiments with which it had begun the assault. More than a thousand Grenadiers had been lost by each of the SS Divisions and this was only the opening battle.

On D-Day for Operation 'Spring Awakening', 6th March 1945, army units crossing the Drau river in a fast motor-boat assault established a bridgehead and drove back the 3rd Bulgarian Division defending the river line. The Panzer Army then made the main thrust between Lake Balaton and the Velence lake, with the first objective of the Leibstandarte and Hitler Youth Divisions of I SS Panzer Corps being to force bridgeheads across the Sio Canal. Despite Hungarian warnings that the ground was marshy and therefore unsuitable for tank operations the attack went ahead. Without preliminary artillery bombardment the SS troops drove into and through fortifications held by Fourth Guards and Twenty-sixth Red Armies. The SS losses were enormous and out of all proportion to the gains made, for, by the end of the day, an advance of only two miles was all that could be recorded. Deep mud and a tenacious defence had destroyed the Panzer thrust and the Army Group Commander's forecast was that future fighting would be of an infantry nature and that this would be heavy, slow and costly. Between Lake Balaton and the Saviz Canal the Leibstandarte then made a four-mile advance but the Russian defence grew as the Red Command moved troops to counter the German blow.

There was bitter fighting at Simontornya and Azora, two towns which the SS needed to hold before they could swing the direction of their advance southwards. The Soviets, equally aware of the importance of those places, were fighting desperately to hold them. By 9th March I and II SS Panzer Corps, with the Leibstandarte in the van, had broken through the CXXXV Red Infantry Corps and had reached the Bozotpatak–Enneying line.

Exhausted by the effort made in such appalling conditions the drive began to falter and the last reserves were committed in an effort to carry the assault forward. Dietrich went up to the advanced positions to spur on the Grenadiers and inspired by the presence of their old commander the Leibstandarte pushed ahead, but II Corps could not keep pace and slowed down the assault although the forward movement was still maintained, resulting, two days later, in the capture of Simontornya and the establishing of a bridgehead across the Sio Canal. The Russians were now throwing in masses of men to halt the advance and the fighting during 12th March reached a peak of ferocity. Not only was Russian resistance increasing but supplies were not reaching the forward Grenadiers. There were shortages in petrol, ammunition and spares and severe losses had reduced the Panzer Army's total strength in tanks and self-propelled guns to only 185 vehicles.

Dietrich, always a realist, asked that the offensive be broken off but his request was overtaken by events when on 16th March the Soviet counter-attack came in. Army Group South regrouped and concentrated the Panzer Army around Stuhlweissenburg, for the direction of the main Russian thrust made it evident that the Red Command intended to strike through that town to seize Vienna. The Russian blow split the Army Group and the plans for a staged, orderly withdrawal had to be abandoned under the fury of Russian fighter-bomber attacks. For two days, 24th and 25th, the SS Panzer Army withdrew westwards trying to hold ninety-three miles of front, between the Danube and Lake Balaton, with only six understrength divisions. By this stage of the fighting the Leibstandarte Division, like all the others, was a division in name only but it was still expected to execute divisional responsibilities and to hold a divisional width of front. Inevitably this meant that there was no continuous line but, instead, a series of strongpoints isolated from central direction. The story of these last weeks of the war is one of rearguards, of handfuls of men fighting and dying in little conflicts against overwhelming odds. But not all the SS were so dedicated. The ranks were being filled by low-calibre recruits; airmen who no longer had aeroplanes to fly or to service, seamen from ships which would never sail against an enemy, combed-out factory workers with no desire to die a hero's death: even conscripts were now serving in the SS. But always there was a leaven of fresh volunteers willing to serve in Adolf Hitler's Bodyguard just as there was a hard core of battle-hardened veterans who had survived the years of war and this leaven proved sufficient to sustain the name that the Leibstandarte had won for itself. About this time Hitler received a report that some of his SS soldiers lacked moral fibre and he convinced himself that his Party troops had failed him miserably in Operation 'Spring Awakening'. Degradation was the only fit punishment. The Sixth SS Panzer Army units were ordered to remove their distinctive cuff titles and some regiments (though not those of the Leibstandarte) complied with the order. Dietrich and most senior officers ignored it, Hitler's 'faithful Sepp' bitterly commenting: 'There's your reward for all you've done these past five years.' In an effort to restore the situation Himmler organized SS cordons in rear areas and flying courts-martial with powers to execute, summarily, deserters and other front-dodgers.

The Panzer Army's withdrawal to the line of the Raab was bogged down in mud and hundreds of vehicles as well as much of the heavy equipment were abandoned or destroyed. The appalling conditions also slowed the drive of the Russian armour and Tolbuchin, the Soviet commander, eager to trap the SS and dissatisfied with the speed of the advance, ordered Sixth Guards Tank Army to force the pace regardless of losses. The Red tank troops obeyed and lost 267 tanks in ten days but the momentum of their thrust carried them across the Austrian frontier. This was a shock to the Austrian population for in February their newspapers had been filled with reports of an offensive which would drive the Soviets back to Russia and now, by the end of March, the military situation had deteriorated to such an extent that the Home Guard, the Volkssturm, was being called up.

Tolbuchin's drive fragmented Army Group South and drove the SS Panzer Army north-westwards and the efforts by a new Army Group Commander to knit the front into a whole proved unsuccessful. In the SS Army sector the Grenadiers were so few in number that a continuous line could not be held. The heavy equipment had not been replaced and petrol shortage threatened to reduce still further the fighting strength. Tank trains were formed to conserve fuel, whereby one or two machines towed a number of others, and by these primitive means sufficient tanks were saved to re-form some of the shattered companies. The final deliveries of tanks from Wiener Neustadt factories were taken over by the Leibstandarte and although Dietrich's remark that Sixth SS Panzer Army was well named for it only had six tanks was not absolutely correct, it did underline the bitter knowledge that the end was in sight. The remaining task of his Army, as Dietrich saw it, was to hold the line so as to cover the flank of the German armies in Czechoslovakia. A report at that time on the condition of Dietrich's army stated:

1st SS Panzer Division	Burnt out. The mass of the Division is with Army HQ
12th SS Division	Severely weakened

3rd SS Division	Only remnants remain
6th SS Division	Weakened
2nd SS Division	Of average strength
356 Infantry Division	One infantry regiment. Part of the artillery and pioneer battalion being rested

With such remnants not much could be done but every man was needed for the defence of Austria and Dietrich put into the line alongside his own Leibstandarte Grenadiers the pupils of the Babenbergerburg military academy. On Easter Saturday, 31st March, part of a Leibstandarte battle group carried out counter-attacks against the advancing Soviets so as to cover the withdrawal of the bulk of the division from Kroatisch Geresdorf to Branbergbanys. At Nikitsch a rearguard of nine SS Grenadiers drove back every Russian attack until they had all fallen and on Easter Sunday a Soviet breakthrough in the Pittental compelled the Leibstandarte to carry out a fighting retreat to the line of the Vulka and Leitha rivers.

At Erlach-Katzelsdorf the Grenadiers and the Military Academy pupils formed a rearguard to defend a bridgehead before rejoining the division which was moving closer to Wiener Neustadt. Small groups of SS men defended the Schneeberg and in Eisenstadt stores were set alight to deny them to the oncoming Soviets. At Oggau eighty SS men and Volkssturm men drove off the Russian tank attacks and in Rechnitz there were house-to-house battles. The men of the Leibstandarte were fighting with desperation to defend the soil of Greater Germany.

By 2nd April the Leibstandarte, now formed into two combat groups, held a line running from Vienna to Wiener Neustadt and for the whole of the following week conducted a skilful disengaging battle against V Guards Tank Corps. Army Group South Commander formed a strategic reserve to halt the Russian drive and the 1st SS

Panzer Division, now reduced to a strength of fifty-seven officers, 229 non-commissioned officers and 1,269 men, with sixteen tanks, was withdrawn from the line for that purpose. The reserve was committed during the third week of April when Russian spearheads threatened St Pölten, and Peiper's combat group, with a strength of only two tanks, held the Soviets on the road between that place and Traisen. The other combat group was twenty-five miles to the east at Hafnerburg. But pressure by Ninth Guards Army forced the Leibstandarte to give ground again, firstly in the direction of St Pölten–Mariazell and then towards Steyr. To cover the retreat in the Mariazell area a battery of SS anti-aircraft gunners was put in as a rearguard and their self-sacrifice enabled the bulk of the division to reach the Enns river. The German Army Group South was now trapped between the Eastern and the Western Allies.

Hitler's death confirmed the belief that the war had only days to run its course and active preparations were made by High Command to end hostilities; but over all the German moves hung the uncertainty of how the SS, and specifically the Leibstandarte, would react to surrender. Would they accept the inevitable and comply with the terms or had they in mind some dramatic, Wagnerian finale? In the event Dietrich decided to follow the general line and with no heroics but with a final, formal parade the bulk of Adolf Hitler's Guard passed into captivity. For some this was the prelude to trials as war criminals and for the great mass it was the start of years to be spent as prisoners of war. To all of them the most bitter humiliation lay in the knowledge that in Allied eyes they were members of a criminal organization and not, as they considered themselves to be, soldiers of élite formations in a first-class army.

7

Personalities

The Leibstandarte had four commanders in its twelve-year history. They were:

17th March 1933–26th July 1943:
SS Obergruppenführer und General der Waffen SS Josef Dietrich.

27th July 1943–20th August 1944:
SS Brigadeführer und Generalmajor der Waffen SS Theodor Wisch.

20th August 1944–6th February 1945:
SS Oberführer Wilhelm Mohnke.

6th February 1945–8th May 1945:
SS Brigadeführer und Generalmajor der Waffen SS Otto Kumm

DIETRICH Josef *SS Oberst-Gruppenführer und Panzer Generaloberst der Waffen SS*

'Sepp' Dietrich was something of an enigma. Was he, as Hitler claimed, 'a man unique, under whose swashbuckling appearance is a serious, conscientious, scrupulous character', or, as Rommel asserted, 'flashy and uncultured, needing an amanuensis to turn his thoughts into readable German'? The answer lies in a combination of these two points of view, the key to his character being found in his background.

Dietrich, known affectionately by his men and friends as 'Sepp', was born on 28th May 1892 in Hawangen,

Upper Bavaria, the son of parents whose humble circumstances meant that, after a rudimentary schooling, Dietrich was destined for the butcher's trade. Not finding this, farm labouring or waitering to his taste, he joined the Army at the age of nineteen, thus embarking upon an unconventional military career which would take him from trooper in the 1st Uhlans to commander of the Sixth SS Panzer Army.

After the outbreak of war in 1914 he transferred to the 42nd Infantry Regiment and later served with some distinction in the 5th Storm Battalion and the 13th Bavarian Tank Detachment – both first-class units. By the end of the war he had risen to the rank of Oberfeldwebel (Sergeant-Major) and had been awarded the Iron Cross I Class.

After the war Dietrich earned a meagre living in such jobs as a foreman in a tobacco factory, a customs officer and a petrol pump attendant. His political career can be said to have begun when he joined the Oberland Freikorps in 1919, taking part in the fighting against Polish annexationists in Silesia and in the Munich Putsch in November 1923 as a confirmed nationalist. Dietrich joined the NSDAP in 1928 (NSDAP No. 89015) and entered SS Sturm I the same year (SS No. 1177), becoming one of Hitler's bodyguards shortly after. From that time on his star was in the ascendant. On 18th November 1929 he was elevated to the rank of SS Standartenführer and helped to organize the SS in southern Bavaria, and less than a year later, as an SS Oberführer, took command of SS Abschnitt Süd. On 14th September 1930 the electorate of Lower Bavaria voted him into the Reichstag where he maintained a mute presence. Dietrich's closeness to Hitler began in those days, the latter often referring to the fact that 'he is one of my oldest companions in the struggle'. He had a very definite influence upon his

Führer, and Dietrich was one of the few who could demand private audiences. On one occasion he even tried to get Hitler to refuse Guderian's resignation – an unusual privilege for a divisional commander.

In 1931 Dietrich became an SS Gruppenführer and in October 1932 chief of SS Oberabschnitt Nord. He was also given command of Hitler's personal bodyguard, and his success and courage in this role made a strong impression upon the Führer. He was, therefore, the man to whom Hitler turned in order to create the Leibstandarte. On 27th November 1933 he also became commander of SS Oberabschnitt Ost, and on 4th July 1934 he achieved the rank appropriate to his responsibility and seniority – SS Obergruppenführer. When war broke out Dietrich, who became a General der Waffen SS, almost inevitably found himself one of the most highly decorated commanders of the German armed forces. On 7th July 1940 he was awarded the Knight's Cross by a grateful Führer, followed by the Oakleaves (31st December 1941), the Swords (16th March 1943) and finally the Diamonds to the Knight's Cross on 6th August 1944 (only twenty-seven were awarded).

On 20th April 1942 Hitler promoted his Guard commander to the newly-created rank of SS Oberst-Gruppenführer und Panzer Generaloberst der Waffen SS (the latter being an honorary title commemorating his service in tanks during the First World War), although he was not immediately informed of this, and only wore the appropriate rank insignia from August 1944 on. Dietrich left his Leibstandarte on 27th July 1943 to command I SS Panzer Corps and was further and finally elevated to the command of Sixth SS Panzer Army on 26th October 1944.

Entering US captivity upon the conclusion of the war, Dietrich was sentenced to twenty-five years' imprisonment by a Military Tribunal on 16th July 1946 for his responsibility in the Malmédy Massacre. However, in October 1955 he was released from Landsberg prison, only to be given a further eighteen-month prison sentence by a German court in May 1957 for his part in the killing of the SA leaders in June 1934. The rest of his life was spent quietly until its end on 21st April 1966.

As his background indicates, 'Sepp' Dietrich was largely devoid of any education and culture. Till the end he remained a sergeant-major type. He was a man who enjoyed his drink, his over-large belly testifying to his propensity for beer. He also enjoyed hunting and motor racing – his skill as a driver being sought after by the Auto Union and Daimler-Benz.

His language was more often than not liberally sprinkled with expletives, and his sense of humour was described by a subordinate as 'always coarse, often vulgar and sometimes foul'. Although no sadist, Dietrich enjoyed a good fight, whether it was in the Munich meeting-halls or upon the battlefield, and he liked to affect an air of bravado. His courage, however, was never in doubt, and, while his orders might contain a degree of brutality towards the enemy not often encountered in soldiers, his concern for, and kindness to, those in trouble around him was often in evidence. In Russia, for example, he was consistently considerate towards the civilian population provided he did not consider them to pose any threat to his division. Although he could order the execution of large numbers of Russians, he also showed an old-fashioned courtesy towards Allied prisoners in the early campaigns, on one occasion entertaining captured British officers after the battle for Esquebeck and presenting them with armbands and flashes as souvenirs.

A US interrogator found that Dietrich reminded him of 'a rather battered bar-tender', and von Rundstedt, while conceding that he was 'decent', was sure that he was also 'stupid'. His intelligence was without doubt limited in certain directions, Steiner recalling: 'I once spent an hour and a half trying to explain a situation to "Sepp" Dietrich with the aid of a map. It was quite useless. He understood nothing at all.' Certainly Hitler exaggerated greatly when he described Dietrich as 'a phenomenon in the class of people like Frundsberg, Ziethen and Seidlitz. He is a Bavarian Wrangel, someone irreplaceable'. In contrast Hausser's damning words were: 'Ordinarily he would make a fair sergeant-major, a better sergeant and a first-class corporal.'

However, there was another side to Hitler's Guard commander, one which justified Goebbels' diary note: 'If we had twenty men like him we wouldn't have to worry at all about the Eastern Front.' While the influence of Paul Hausser upon the whole of the early armed SS should not be underestimated, it remains true that it was under Dietrich that the Leibstandarte developed into one of Germany's foremost fighting units. In Hitler's words: 'The role of "Sepp" Dietrich is unique. I have always given him the opportunity to intervene in sore spots. He is a man who is simultaneously cunning, energetic and brutal . . . And what care he takes of his troops!' He was a leader of men rather than a commander, and there can be no doubt that he excelled in this role at the head of Hitler's Guard. Many have testified to his personal charisma, something which photographs of the small pot-bellied man cannot convey. General Eberbach was so impressed with Dietrich's leadership qualities under the strenuous conditions of Normandy 1944, that he exclaimed, 'Dietrich is something grand!'.

One SS officer wrote: ' "Sepp" is all things to us. First and foremost he is a leader, of that there can be no doubt – one of the best . . . He is a father-figure. He has never lost his NCO attitude to his men. For example, when presenting medals other generals walk up and down the ranks with a solemnity that would do justice to a pall-bearer. Not so Dietrich. He looks at the men as if he knows them personally, adjusts a cap, pushes in a stomach, comments on this and that, and generally acts in a way that tells us that we are individual men not just numbers . . . He can be hard on us, but seemingly never without justification. The other day he saw a patrol that had just come off duty, the men tired, dirty and hungry, looking for nothing except food and sleep. One man, however, had slung his rifle in a manner Dietrich cannot abide. That was that. Dietrich had that man doing press-ups, sit-ups, the lot, for over half an hour, and he supervised it all. After it was over the man looked half dead and Dietrich sent him on his way with a bar of chocolate!'

In the light of this the eulogy of the SS propagandist in 1941 appears not to be exaggerated: 'Dietrich the commander, as the father of his men, as the model for his unit commanders, is a hard soldier with a strange tender heart for his comrades.' Such was the man with whom the name of the Leibstandarte is indissolubly linked.

KRAAS Hugo *SS Brigadeführer und Generalmajor der Waffen SS*

Born on 24th January 1911 in Witten, Ruhr, Kraas – the son of a teacher – entered the Leibstandarte in 1935 as an SS Untersturmführer, after completing his military service. During the Polish campaign, as an SS Obersturmführer and a platoon commander in the Anti-tank Company, he was awarded the Iron Cross II Class. In France, as SS Hauptsturmführer and commander of the Motor Cycle Company, Kraas became the first soldier of the campaign to win the Iron Cross I Class.

His good service with the Leibstandarte continued throughout the Greek and Russian campaigns, and he was awarded the German Cross in Gold towards the end of 1941. On 30th March 1943 Kraas, by now an SS Sturmbannführer and commander of the 1st Battalion of the 2nd SS Panzer Grenadier Regiment, was awarded the Knight's Cross. This was followed on 24th January 1944 by the Oakleaves when he was an SS Obersturmbannführer and commander of the regiment.

Transferred from the Leibstandarte, Kraas took over command of the 12th SS Panzer Division 'Hitler Jugend' on 9th November 1944 with the rank of SS Standartenführer, in which position he continued till the end of the war, subsequently reaching the rank of SS Brigadeführer und Generalmajor der Waffen SS. In May 1945 he disappeared and, as far as is known, has not been heard of since. An able leader, he performed particularly well in combat, winning both the Infantry Assault Badge and the Close Combat Clasp.

KUMM Otto *SS Brigadeführer und Generalmajor der Waffen SS*

Kumm was in many ways the typical Waffen SS commander – young, dedicated, able and hard. Born on 1st October 1909 in Hamburg, he left school at eighteen to join the Verfügungstruppe Setzer, joined the NSDAP in 1931 (NSDAP No. 421230) and the SS in the same year (SS No. 18727). On 15th February 1934 he was promoted to SS Untersturmführer, and in 1936 became an SS Hauptsturmführer in the newly formed SS-VT formation – SS Standarte 'Der Führer'.

During the Western campaign he was awarded the Iron Cross I and II classes, and served as a battalion commander. After excellent service in Russia, Kumm was elevated to the rank of SS Obersturmbannführer and the position of commander of the regiment 'Der Führer' in January 1942. Kumm led his unit in heavy fighting in temperatures below −50 degrees Centigrade, and gained a reputation for toughness as well as the award, on 24th February, of the Knight's Cross. When relieved, Kumm's regiment consisted of just thirty-five men – all that had survived the bitter defensive battles against the attacking Soviet forces. His continuing exploits earned him the Oakleaves on 6th April 1943, and shortly after, with the rank of SS Standartenführer, he became Chief of Staff of the 5th SS Panzer Grenadier Division 'Viking'. His abilities caused Kumm to be promoted to SS Oberführer, taking command of the 7th SS Freiwilligen-Gebirgs Division 'Prinz Eugen' on 1st August 1944, and on 9th November he attained the rank of SS Brigadeführer und Generalmajor der Waffen SS.

On 6th February 1945 Kumm came to the Leibstandarte as its new and last commander, winning the Swords to his Knight's Cross on 4th April 1945. A month later he went into captivity along with the remnants of his division which he had contrived to keep fighting until the last.

MEYER Kurt *SS Oberführer*

'Panzer' Meyer was one of those for whom the armed SS provided 'a career open to talent', and by the end of the war he had become one of Germany's best-known soldiers.

Born on 23rd December 1910 in Jerxheim, Meyer was the son of a labourer, with a consequently limited horizon. After an elementary education, he became first a miner and then, in 1929, entered the Mecklenburg Land Police. A supporter of National Socialism (NSDAP No. 316714) from 1930, he joined the SS (SS No. 17559), becoming an

SS Untersturmführer on 10th July 1932. He entered the Leibstandarte early in 1934, being promoted SS Obersturmführer on 10th March 1935 and SS Hauptsturmführer on 12th September 1937. Serving well in Poland and France he first revealed his military prowess when, as an SS Sturmbannführer and commander of the Reconnaissance Detachment, he stormed through the heavily defended Klissura Pass in Greece at the head of his unit. In two days Meyer's unorthodox but brilliant leadership had resulted in the capture of some 12,000 men and two key points, and for this he received the Knight's Cross on 15th May 1941.

Meyer's star was now in the ascendant, and his reputation increased considerably during the advance into Russia when his unit spearheaded the Leibstandarte with such *élan* that he became known as 'Der schnelle Meyer'. Promoted SS Obersturmbannführer, his exploits at Kharkov earned him more fame and, on 23rd February 1943, the Oakleaves. Further promotion occurred in July when, upon being transferred to command the newly-formed 25th SS Panzer Grenadier Regiment of the 12th SS Panzer Grenadier Division 'Hitler Jugend', he was made SS Standartenführer. His energetic work helped to mould this inexperienced collection of German youth into a formidable fighting force which provided tough opposition for the Allies in Normandy. There Meyer was in command of a battle group which took part in particularly tough battles against the Canadians around Caen. Upon the death of Witt, Meyer assumed control of the 12th SS Division on 16th June 1944, and two weeks later on 1st August, at the age of thirty-three, he was promoted SS Oberführer – he was now the youngest of the senior SS officers and of the divisional commanders throughout the armed forces. For his exploits in the fierce Normandy battle (his division lost 60 per cent of its strength in casualties by 11th July), Meyer was awarded the Swords to the Knight's Cross on 26th August. He was captured on 6th September near Amiens.

After the war he was tried as the first German war criminal and found guilty of the murder of forty-five Canadian prisoners on 8th June 1944, being sentenced to life imprisonment. But on 7th September 1954 he was released, and became an active member of HIAG – the Waffen SS Old Comrades Association – until his death on 23rd December 1961. In 1951 he published his memoirs of service in the Waffen SS, entitled simply *Grenadiere*.

MOHNKE Wilhelm *SS Brigadeführer und Generalmajor der Waffen SS*

Mohnke, the third commander of the Leibstandarte, was born in Lübeck on 15th March 1911, and joined the NSDAP (NSDAP No. 649684) and the SS (SS No. 15541) in 1931. On 28th June 1933 he was promoted to SS Untersturmführer in the Leibstandarte and four months later to SS Hauptsturmführer. He had risen to the rank of SS Obersturmbannführer by mid-1943. Transferred to the 12th SS Division 'Hitler Jugend', he commanded the SS Panzer Grenadier Regiment No. 26 during the battle for Normandy and received the Knight's Cross on 20th July 1944.

On the 20th August he took over command of the Leibstandarte from the wounded Wisch with the rank of SS Standartenführer. He was promoted SS Oberführer on 4th November. Leading the division in the Ardennes, Mohnke was transferred to Berlin on 6th February 1945 with the rank of SS Brigadeführer und Generalmajor der Waffen SS to become Commandant of the Reich Chancellery. His battle group fought to the end in the area of the Führer Bunker, and Mohnke successfully escaped after Hitler's death. He was released from Soviet captivity in October 1955. An ardent National Socialist, Mohnke proved himself a tough commander in the field.

PEIPER Jochen *SS Obersturmbannführer*

Peiper has been described as 'one of the most dashing German officers of the war', and certainly his exploits during the Ardennes offensive would seem to prove it. Perhaps more than any other man Peiper was the epitome of the Waffen SS officer corps, combining a daredevil *élan* in battle with military efficiency of the highest order.

Born on 30th January 1915 in Berlin of a military family, Jochen Peiper entered the Leibstandarte (SS No. 132496) in 1934 and became SS Untersturmführer on 20th May 1936 after having passed out of SS Junkerschule Braunschweig. After a spell of duty with his unit he became Adjutant to the Reichsführer SS. When the war started Peiper was a company commander, and fought well in Poland and France, being awarded the Iron Cross, in both classes. After having served ably in Greece and Russia, Peiper was promoted to SS Sturmbannführer in mid-1942 and was appointed to command the 3rd Battalion of the 2nd SS Panzer Regiment. On 6th April 1943 he was awarded the Knight's Cross, and in November of that year he rose to command the 1st SS Panzer Regiment with the rank of SS Obersturmbannführer. He received the Oakleaves on 21st January 1944.

It was in the Ardennes offensive that Peiper ensured for himself a place in history, the nature of which is two-fold. First there was his role as commander of a battle group, one which tested his fighting ability and powers of leadership to the full, and which gained him the Swords to his Knight's Cross on 28th December 1944. Secondly there was his part in the indiscriminate killings in which his unit featured, the most notable being the Malmédy Massacre, for which he was condemned to death by a US Tribunal on 16th July 1946. He was, however, released on 22nd December 1956 after his sentence had been commuted to life imprisonment five years earlier.

WISCH Theodor *SS Brigadeführer und Generalmajor der Waffen SS*

Born on 13th December 1907 in Wesselburener Hoog, 'Teddy' Wisch was one of the early members of the SS (SS No. 4759), joining the NSDAP in late 1930 (NSDAP No. 369050) and becoming one of the original 120 members of the Leibstandarte in March 1933 after finishing his studies in agriculture. On 28th July 1933 he was promoted to SS Untersturmführer, and on 1st October of that year became an SS Hauptsturmführer. He led his company in the Polish campaign, winning the Iron Cross I and II classes, and as an SS Sturmbannführer and Commander of the 2nd Battalion he served in France, Greece and Russia, being awarded the Knight's Cross on 15th September 1941. In June 1942 Wisch became Commander of the 2nd SS Panzer Grenadier Regiment, earning the German Cross in Gold after Kharkov.

On 27th July 1943, as an SS Brigadeführer und Generalmajor der Waffen SS, Wisch emerged to prominence as Commander of Hitler's Guard in succession to Dietrich. Aged only thirty-six, he proved himself capable of filling the vacuum left by his predecessor – no mean task. Although he had not the personal charisma of Dietrich, Wisch nevertheless retained the affection and confidence of his men, proving himself an able commander. On 12th December 1944 he was awarded the Oakleaves, followed on 28th August 1945 by the Swords to the Knight's Cross. He was, however, badly wounded in the bitter Normandy fighting on 20th August and command was transferred to Mohnke.

WITT Fritz *SS Brigadeführer und Generalmajor der Waffen SS*

Along with Mohnke and Wisch, Fritz Witt was one of the few original Leibstandarte members to achieve high command and a reputation. Born on 25th May 1908 in Höhenlimburg, Witt joined the SS (SS No. 21518) and the Party (NSDAP No. 816769) in 1931, becoming an SS Untersturmführer on 1st September 1933. Promoted to SS Obersturmführer on 9th May 1934, he was transferred from the Leibstandarte in 1935 to become a company commander in the SS Standarte 'Deutschland' – another SS-VT formation. In 1939 as an SS Hauptsturmführer, he won the Iron Cross I and II classes in Poland, and in October he took over command of the 1st Battalion of 'Deutschland' with the rank of SS Sturmbannführer. He was awarded the Knight's Cross on 4th September 1940 for his service in the French campaign.

In October 1940 Witt returned to his old unit as a battalion commander. The campaign in Russia was for him a time of great personal achievement in battle, and he was awarded the German Cross in Gold, the Infantry Assault Badge, and, finally, the Oakleaves on 1st March 1943. In June 1942 he was given the special task of forming the 1st SS Panzer Grenadier Regiment, and as an SS Standartenführer he commanded the unit with great success. After Kharkov, owing to his excellent powers of organization and leadership, Witt was chosen to command and mould into a fighting unit the 'Crack Babies' of the 12th SS Division 'Hitler Jugend'. Promotion to SS Brigadeführer und Generalmajor der Waffen SS came on 1st July 1943, Witt at the age of thirty-five thus becoming the second youngest general in Germany's armed forces. His success as a commander can be measured by the battle-readiness and ability shown by his young and inexperienced division during the Normandy fighting. As a result of his habit of leading his men personally and of being where the action was hottest, Witt was killed in action during the battle for Caen on 16th June 1944. Upon hearing of the death of his former comrade Dietrich exclaimed: 'That's one of the best gone. He was too good a soldier to stay alive for long.'

WITTMANN Michael *SS Obersturmführer*

Wittmann was without doubt the foremost tank commander of the Second World War (indeed, any war), a man of whom Dietrich said: 'He was a fighter in every way, he lived and breathed action.' Born on 22nd April 1914 in Vogethal, Upper Palatinate, Wittmann gave up a career in agriculture in 1937 to enter the Leibstandarte. By the outbreak of the war he was an SS Unterscharführer, and commanded an armoured car in Poland and France. He earned the Iron Cross II Class in Greece while in charge of an assault gun, and the I Class during the advance to Rostov in 1941, after having been wounded twice. He was then sent to the SS Junkerschule Bad Tölz and, in December 1942, was promoted to Untersturmführer.

Upon rejoining the Leibstandarte, Wittmann was made section commander in the 13th (Heavy) Company of the 1st SS Panzer Regiment. Now, in the turret of his Tiger, his outstanding achievement was to begin. His crew – Woll, Berger, Kirschner and Pollmann (Woll later won the Knight's Cross) – were a first-class combination of tankmen. During the Battle of Kursk, Wittmann's tank knocked out thirty Soviet tanks, twenty-eight anti-tank guns and two artillery batteries. By 9th January 1944 the score was sixty-six tanks, and for this he was awarded on the 13th the Knight's Cross. On that day, as if to celebrate, he shot up nineteen T34s and three heavy assault guns. On the 20th he was promoted to SS Obersturmführer and ten days later received the Oakleaves. In April he became a company commander of the Heavy Panzer Battalion 501 of the Leibstandarte Panzer Corps. He led his Tigers against the Allies in Normandy, taking part in the particularly heavy fighting around Caen. His last and most famous action was on Height 213 on 13th June when, in one of the most brilliant individual exploits of the war, Wittmann held up and practically destroyed 22nd Brigade of the British 7th Armoured Division and added twenty-five to his tally. Nine days later he was awarded the Swords to his Knight's Cross. He was killed in action south of Caen on 8th August 1944. His final score, achieved in under two years, amounted to no less than 138 tanks and assault guns and 132 anti-tank guns. As 'Panzer' Meyer wrote: 'Michael Wittmann died as he had lived – brave, dashing and a living example to his Grenadiers.'

WÜNSCHE Max *SS Obersturmbannführer*

Wünsche was an outstanding young officer whose Waffen SS career can in no way be faulted. Born on 20th April 1914 at Kittlitz near Lobau, he joined the SS-VT at the age of twenty (SS No. 153508). His military talents were soon recognized and he was sent to SS Junkerschule Bad Tölz, becoming an SS Untersturmführer upon his birthday in 1936. He was there to become a typical product of the SS training system, his later bravery and dash in action nearly costing him his life on more than one occasion.

After some service in the Leibstandarte he was appointed an aide-de-camp to the Führer, accompanying

him to Poland. However much of an honour that might
have been, Wünsche was glad when he returned to his
unit in time to command a company in France. During
the brief campaign he was wounded and was awarded
both classes of the Iron Cross. In the Balkans his efficiency and energy resulted in his serving in the demanding
position of Adjutant, with the rank of SS Hauptsturmführer, a post which obviously marked him out for future
advancement. After having commanded the Assault Gun
Detachment in Russia in 1941 he was sent to the War
Academy, from which he emerged in late 1942 as an SS
Sturmbannführer to take command of the newly formed
1st Battalion of the 1st SS Panzer Regiment. His excellent
service earned him the German Cross in Gold and, on
28th February 1943, the Knight's Cross as well as further
promotion to SS Obersturmbannführer.

In July 1943, along with other first-rate Leibstandarte
officers, Wünsche was transferred to the 12th SS Division
'Hitler Jugend', where, at the age of twenty-eight, he
became commander of the 12th SS Panzer Regiment. His
efforts were such that this newly formed unit became one
of the foremost on the Normandy front, destroying 250
enemy tanks in eight weeks. On the 11th August 1944,
Wünsche received the Oakleaves to his Knight's Cross,
and his achievements would no doubt have continued had
he not been badly wounded and captured during the
Battle for the Falaise Gap.

Appendix 1
Ranks of the Waffen SS with British and US equivalents

Waffen SS	Britain	USA
SS Oberst- Gruppenführer und Generaloberst der Waffen SS*	Field-Marshal	General of Army (5 stars)
	General	General (4 stars)
SS Obergruppenführer und General der Waffen SS**		
SS Gruppenführer und Generalleutnant der Waffen SS**	Lieutenant-General	Lieutenant-General (3 stars)
SS Brigadeführer und Generalmajor der Waffen SS**	Major-General	Major-General (2 stars)
	Brigadier	Brigadier-General (1 star)
SS Oberführer		
SS Standartenführer	Colonel	Colonel
SS Obersturmbannführer	Lieutenant-Colonel	Lieutenant-Colonel
SS Sturmbannführer	Major	Major
SS Hauptsturmführer	Captain	Captain
SS Obersturmführer	Lieutenant	First Lieutenant
SS Untersturmführer	Second-Lieutenant	Second-Lieutenant
SS Sturmscharführer	Warrant Officer 1st Class (RSM)	Sergeant-Major
SS Hauptscharführer	Warrant Officer 2nd Class (CSM etc.)	1st and Master Sergeant
SS Oberscharführer	Quartermaster-Sergeant (RQMS/CQMS etc.)	Technical-Sergeant
SS Scharführer	Staff-Sergeant	Staff-Sergeant
SS Unterscharführer	Sergeant	Sergeant
SS Rottenführer	Corporal	Corporal
SS Sturmann	Lance-Corporal	Acting Corporal
SS Oberschütze		Private 1st Class
SS Mann,*** SS Schütze, SS Panzerschütze etc.	Private, Rifleman etc.	Private etc.

*Rank introduced on 7th April 1942.

**Waffen SS rank introduced in late 1940.

***Discontinued during the war.

No precise equivalent can be given in every case, especially with those of General rank.

Appendix 2
Select Bibliography

d'ALQUEN, Gunther, *Die SS: Geschichte, Aufgabe und Organization.*

BAUER, Eddy, *Panzer Krieg* (2 volumes), Verlag Offene Worte, Verleger Bodo Zimmermann, Bonn, 1965.

BEST, Werner, *Die deutsche Polizei.*

BEST, Walther, *Mit der Leibstandarte im Westen.*

BOVY, Marcel, *Bataille de l'Amblève*, Editions – Les Amitiés Musanes, Liège, 1950.

BUCHHEIM, H., *Anatomie des SS Staates*, Deutscher Taschenbuch Verlag, Munich, 1967.

FEY, Will, *Panzer*, J. Lehmann Verlag, Munich, 1960.

GORLITZ, *Die Waffen SS.*

GOSZTONY, Peter, *Endkampf an der Donau*, Verlag Fritz Molden, Vienna, 1969.

GUDERIAN, Heinz, *Achtung Panzer*, Union Deutsche, Stuttgart, ND.

GUDERIAN, Heinz, *Mit den Panzern im Ost und West*, Volk und Reich Verlag, Göttingen, 1953.

HAUSSER, Paul, *Soldaten wie andere auch*, Munin Verlag, 1966.

HAUSSER, Paul, *Waffen SS im Einsatz*, Plesse Verlag, Göttingen, 1953.

HÖHNE, Heinz, *The Order of the Death's Head*, Pan Books, 1971.

KOGON, Egon, *Der SS Staat*, Bermann-Fischer, Stockholm, 1947.

KRÄTSCHMER, E. G., *Die Ritterkreuzträger der Waffen SS*, Plesse Verlag, Göttingen, 1957.

LEHERY, *Défaite allemande à l'est.*

MAARTZ, Josef, *Luxembourg in der Rundstedt Offensive*, Skt. Paulus Drückerei, Ardennes, 1948.

MANSTEIN, Erich, *Lost Victories*, Methuen, London, 1958.

MELLENTHIN, Friedrich Wilhelm, *Panzerschlachten, 1939–1945*, Vowinckel Verlag, Neckargemünd, 1963.

MEYER, Kurt, *Grenadiere*, Schild Verlag, Munich, 1957.

MOLLO, Andrew, *Uniforms of the SS*, Vols I, III, VI, Historical Research Unit, London, various dates.

OGORKIEWICZ, Richard M., *Armour*, Stevens, London, 1960.

O. K. W. *Sieg im Westen*, 1940.

RAUCHENSTEINER, Manfried, *Krieg in Österreich*, Österreichischer Bundesverlag für Unterricht, Wissenschaft und Kunst, Vienna, 1970.

REITLINGER, Gerald, *The SS – Alibi of a Nation*, Heinemann, London, 1956.

ROSSIWALL, Theodore, *Die letzten Tage*, Kremayr and Scheriau, Vienna, 1969.

STEIN, George, *The Waffen SS*, Oxford University Press, 1966.

STEINER, Felix, *Die Freiwilligen: Idee und Opfergang*, Plesse Verlag, Göttingen, 1958.

Official and Semi-Official Works

British
   The History of the Second World War (series)

ELLIS, L. F., *The War in France and Flanders*, HMSO, London, 1953.

PLAYFAIR, I. S. (Major-General), *The Mediterranean and the Middle East*, HMSO, 1954.

ELLIS, L. F., *Victory in the West* (2 vols), HMSO, London, 1968.

198 *Select Bibliography*

Dutch
Die Strijd of Nederlands Grondgebied, Tijdens de Wereldoolog. II.

German
Arbeitskreis für Wehrforschung, *Kriegstagebuch des OKW*, Bernard & Graefe, Frankfurt, 1965.
Keilig, *Das Heer* (3 vols), Verlag Hans-Henning, Podzun, Bad Nauheim, various dates.

Die Wehrmacht im Kampf (series)
VORMANN, Nicolaus von, *Tcherkassy*, No. 3 of the series, Vowinckel, Heidelberg, 1954.
STEETS, Hans, *Uman*, No. 4 of the series, Vowinckel, Heidelberg, 1955.
STEETS, Hans, *Kuban–Sevastopol*, No. 7, Vowinckel, Heidelberg, 1955.
STEETS, Hans, *Die nogaische Steppe*, No. 8, Vowinckel, Heidelberg, 1956.
HOTH, Hermann, *Panzer Operationen*, No. 11, Vowinckel, Heidelberg, 1956.
BUCHNER, Alex, *Der deutsche Griechenland Feldzug*, No. 14, Vowinckel, Heidelberg, 1957.
STEETS, Hans, *Zwischen Dnieper und Don*, No. 15, Vowinckel, Heidelberg, 1957.
MUNZEL, Oskar, *Panzer Taktik*, No. 20, Vowinckel, Heidelberg, 1959.

Polish
Komisa Historycz Polskiego, *Polskie zely B orajne w Drugiej Wojnie Swiatowej*, Sikorski Institute, London, 1951.

New Zealand
McCLYMONT, W. G., *New Zealand in the Second World War: To Greece*, Whitcombe and Tombs, Christchurch, NZ, 1959.

Russia
Istoriya velikoi otechestvennoi Voynni Sovetskovo Soyussa, Moscow, 1961–64.

United States
US Army Official Series
HARRISON, G. A., *Cross Channel Attack*, Office of the Chief of the Military History Department of the Army, Washington, DC, 1951.

BLUMENSON, Martin, *Breakout and Pursuit*, Office of the Chief etc., Washington, DC, 1961.

COLE, Hugh M., *Ardennes and the Battle of the Bulge*, Office of the Chief etc., Washington, DC, 1965.

US War Department, *Armoured Breakthrough*, Washington, DC, 1946.

US War Department, *Report of Operations, 1st Army*, ND.

XX Corps Association, *XX Corps*, Mainichi Publishing Co., Ltd, Osaka, Japan.

HEWITT, Robert L., *Work Horse of the Western Front: The Story of 30th Infantry Division*, Infantry Press, Washington, 1946.

RUBEL, George K., *Daredevil Tankers: The Story of 740 Battalion*, ND.

Various historical studies produced by the US Army, divisional, regimental and Army histories.

Index